YORK NOTES

Anne Frank

The Diary of a Young Girl

Note by Bernard Haughey

 Longman   York Press

Bernard Haughey is hereby identified as author of this work in accordance with
Section 77 of the Copyright, Designs and Patents Act 1988

YORK PRESS
322 Old Brompton Road, London SW5 9JH

PEARSON EDUCATION LIMITED
Edinburgh Gate, Harlow,
Essex CM20 2JE, United Kingdom
Associated companies, branches and representatives throughout the world

First published 2001

ISBN 0-582-43178-6

Designed by Vicki Pacey
Phototypeset by Gem Graphics, Trenance, Mawgan Porth, Cornwall
Colour reproduction and film output by Spectrum Colour
Produced by Addison Wesley Longman China Limited, Hong Kong

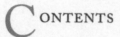CONTENTS

PREFACE

York Notes are designed to give you a broader perspective on works of literature studied at GCSE and equivalent levels. We have carried out extensive research into the needs of the modern literature student prior to publishing this new edition. Our research showed that no existing series fully met students' requirements. Rather than present a single authoritative approach, we have provided alternative viewpoints, empowering students to reach their own interpretations of the text. York Notes provide a close examination of the work and include biographical and historical background, summaries, glossaries, analyses of characters, themes, structure and language, cultural connections and literary terms.

If you look at the Contents page you will see the structure for the series. However, there's no need to read from the beginning to the end as you would with a novel, play, poem or short story. Use the Notes in the way that suits you. Our aim is to help you with your understanding of the work, not to dictate how you should learn.

York Notes are written by English teachers and examiners, with an expert knowledge of the subject. They show you how to succeed in coursework and examination assignments, guiding you through the text and offering practical advice. Questions and comments will extend, test and reinforce your knowledge. Attractive colour design and illustrations improve clarity and understanding, making these Notes easy to use and handy for quick reference.

York Notes are ideal for:
- Essay writing
- Exam preparation
- Class discussion

The author of this Note is Bernard Haughey, a former head of English who has taught in a variety of technical colleges, grammar and comprehenive schools. He was an examiner for a major O' level examination board and is the author of York Notes on Charles Dickens' *David Copperfield* and Robert Bolt's *A Man for all Seasons*.

The text used in these Notes is the 1997 Penguin Books definitive edition, edited by Otto Frank and Mirjam Pressler.

Health Warning: This study guide will enhance your understanding, but should not replace the reading of the original text and/or study in class.

PART ONE

INTRODUCTION

HOW TO STUDY A NOVEL

You have bought this book because you wanted to study a novel on your own. This may supplement classwork.

- You will need to read the novel several times. Start by reading it quickly for pleasure, then read it slowly and carefully. Further readings will generate new ideas and help you to memorise the details of the story.
- Make careful notes on themes, plot and characters of the novel. The plot will change some of the characters. Who changes?
- The novel may not present events chronologically. Does the novel you are reading begin at the beginning of the story or does it contain flashbacks and a muddled time sequence? Can you think why?
- How is the story told? Is it narrated by one of the characters or by an all-seeing ('omniscient') narrator?
- Does the same person tell the story all the way through? Or do we see the events through the minds and feelings of a number of different people?
- Which characters does the narrator like? Which characters do you like or dislike? Do your sympathies change during the course of the book? Why? When?
- Any piece of writing (including your notes and essays) is the result of thousands of choices. No book had to be written in just one way: the author could have chosen other words, other phrases, other characters, other events. How could the author of your novel have written the story differently? If events were recounted by a minor character how would this change the novel?

Studying on your own requires self-discipline and a carefully thought-out work plan in order to be effective. Good luck.

Family
background

Annalies Marie Frank was born of a Jewish family in Frankfurt am Main, Germany, on 12 June 1929. Her sister, Margot Betty, was at that time three years old. Her father, Otto, came from a well-to-do family who had lived in Frankfurt for hundreds of years. Her mother, Edith, came from the German town of Aachen, near the frontier with Holland.

Otto's father had founded a bank. Unfortunately, the stock market crash placed this bank in a difficult position, from which it never really recovered, so that Otto and his family, although reasonably well-off and well respected, were not enormously wealthy.

When Adolf Hitler became Chancellor of Germany in 1933 Otto understood that it was now an urgent necessity to remove his Jewish family from Germany. The German government's campaign, urging the boycott of Jewish businesses, convinced him that the time was ripe to accept an offer of work in Amsterdam. Anti-Jewish bias had crept into education, too, adding

Leaving Germany further impetus to the decision of the Franks to leave Germany.

In 1933, Otto left for Amsterdam to arrange accommodation for his family. His wife and daughters went to live temporarily with Edith's mother in Aachen. Later the same year, Edith and Margot joined Otto, leaving Anne with her grandmother. Their new home was a third-floor apartment in a modern block.

When Anne eventually arrived in Amsterdam, she attended the pre-school section of a Montessori school, though Margot went to a more traditional establishment. Margot was a particularly successful pupil; Anne's only difficulties lay in maths and an inability to stop chattering. The Franks were a very hospitable family and neighbours' children were always around their house.

Otto's business   In the absence of Otto, who was compelled to travel
extensively throughout Holland in the course of his
work, Victor Kugler took charge of the office and was
ably assisted by Miep Gies who was originally from
Austria but had chosen to stay with her foster parents
in Holland. Both these people became true friends of
the Franks, who eventually entrusted their lives to
them.

Otto began to operate a second company, providing
spices for sausage producers. His friend, Johannes
Kleiman, was a company director assisted by Hermann
van Pels, who was an expert in this field. The van Pels
family became close friends of the Franks. In the diary,
van Pels is known as van Daan. Otto's businesses were
doing well and he moved into new premises at 263
Prinsengrast, the building that later disguised the Secret
Annexe. In order to prevent his businesses being
appropriated by the Nazis, Otto had his Pectacon firm
transferred to Victor Kugler and Miep Gies under a
new name. Later, his Opekta firm became Gies and
Company with Kleiman as managing director.

On 12 June 1942, Anne's thirteenth birthday, she was
given her red notebook with the tartan cover and little
lock that was to hold the closest secrets of her soul and
give the world a fascinating insight into a young girl's
feelings as she moved towards maturity. It was only in
this diary that she could be openly frank and freely
express her every thought and emotion.

The Franks' life changed suddenly and dramatically
when Margot received a summons to the Central Office
for Jewish Emigration and the decision was made to
escape to the hiding place which they had been
preparing for this purpose. Apart from the last chapter
of her history, Anne's remaining story is the substance
of her Diary of a Young Girl.

After the Annexe On 4 August, 1944 the occupants of the Annexe, along with Kugler and Kleiman (who both survived the war) were arrested; their hiding place had been betrayed to the authorities. On 3 September 1944, all eight occupants of the Annexe were bundled aboard a cattle truck on the last train to leave for the notorious Auschwitz concentration camp in Poland, a journey that took two days. The men were then separated from the women. Hermann van Pels (van Daan) died in the gas chamber, Fritz Pfeffer (Dussel) in Neuengamme concentration camp. Edith died in Auschwitz in January 1945. Peter van Pels (van Daan) died in Mauthausen concentration camp in May and Mrs van Pels (van Daan) died in Theresianstadt or thereabouts around the same time. At the end of October, Margot and Anne were transferred to Bergen-Belsen concentration camp where, emaciated and neglected, they died of typhus a few weeks before British troops liberated the camp in April 1945. Otto, alone, was to survive the war. He died in 1980 at the age of ninety-one.

Miep was not arrested and rescued Anne's diary, which she gave to Otto after the war. He had it published in 1947. Since then, it has been printed in fifty-five languages and has become a world best-seller. The reader may be confused by the changes of names with the diary names in brackets; Otto altered some original names before publication in order to spare their families any possible distress.

CONTEXT & SETTING

To understand the conditions which brought Anne Frank and millions of other innocent people to their deaths in Europe in the 1930s and 1940s, it is necessary to have some knowledge of how these conditions were created.

There had been great unrest in Germany since the end of the First World War. A humiliating peace treaty (Treaty of Versailles) had been imposed on the defeated nation demanding crippling payments to France and Belgium, which led to friction between those countries and Germany and resulted in strikes and hyper-inflation in Germany. Millions faced starvation. Social unrest was high and attempts at revolution many. Democracy seemed to have failed the German people.

Hitler and Nazi rule

The National Socialist Party (Nazi Party), led by Adolf Hitler, then began to gain support. On becoming Chancellor in 1933, he immediately assumed the powers of a dictator. All opposition was mercilessly crushed. Communists were arrested in droves; trades unions and all political parties, except the Nazi Party, were abolished. The army had to swear an oath of allegiance to Adolf Hitler, now called the Fuhrer. By 1934, he had destroyed all opposition within his own party by ruthlessly murdering 400 potentially dissident members in 'The Night of the Long Knives'.

Now that Hitler had complete control, he could put into practice his theory that the Germans were a 'master race' and was able to indulge his ingrained hatred of the Jews. Added to this was his desire to create a German empire in Europe, which was clearly evident from the way he had set about subjugating state after state. In Nazi Germany, the Jews had lost the right to vote, concentration camps were being established and numerous restrictions against Jews were being imposed. Many immigrant Jews lived in the area of Amsterdam in which the Franks had settled; generally, Jews in Holland were integrated into the

Oppression of Jews

community and under no threat from the Dutch. Jewish firms in Germany were being transferred to German ownership and Hitler considered Holland to be a Germanic state. It can easily be seen how the safety of the Frank family in Holland was under an imminent threat.

Nazi rule in Holland

The German attack on Poland on 1 September 1939 increased Dutch fears of an invasion of Holland. These fears were realised when German troops crossed the Dutch border on 10 May 1940. There had been no declaration of war and within five days Holland had surrendered. Restrictive regulations were gradually introduced into Holland by the Germans: Jews were required to register with the authorities; people were forbidden, under pain of fines or imprisonment, to listen to any radio broadcasts not approved by the Nazis; Jews were forbidden to go to cinemas, swimming pools, hotels, beaches and parks and all kinds of transport, public and private, were denied them. They were also required to wear a yellow star prominently on their clothing to distinguish them from the rest of the population. Added to all this was the nightly curfew. The arbitrary arrest of many Jews provoked a general strike led by the Communists, which was put down with great ferocity by the German authorities. From 1941 onwards, Jewish children were obliged to attend Jewish schools.

These were the circumstances at the time when Anne wrote her diary, throughout which references to the war and local persecution abound. The threat of instant arrest and summary execution are at all times present and provide a back-cloth of fear that permeates the entire diary. News regularly reaches their ears of the arrest of their friends and neighbours and of deportations to Germany or to unknown destinations in eastern Europe. The break-ins they experience are themselves a symptom of the breakdown of law and order caused by war, foreign occupation and deprivation.

In this way, the internal dramas of their lives are put into perspective by the ever-present terror of extinction. This is the inevitable nature of the circumstances in which the diary is written and the context in which we see Anne's development towards maturity which, sadly, never reaches its fulfilment.

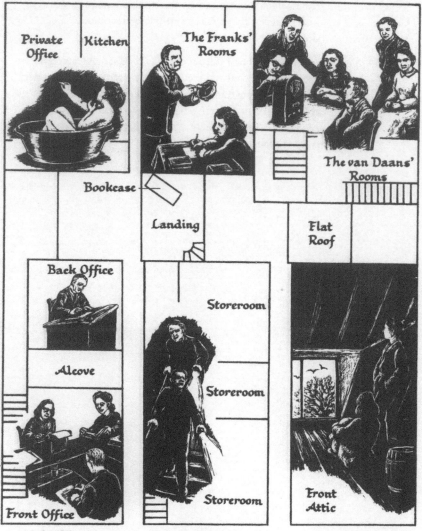

Mrs van Daan

Mr van Daan

Mr Frank

Mrs Frank

Anne Frank

OPEKTA GIES & CO

Mr Dussel

Margot Frank

Bep Voskuijl

Miep Gies

Jan Gies

Mr Voskuijl

Mr Kleiman

Mr Kugler

Part two

Summaries

General summary

Anne saw her diary as her friend, Kitty, in whom she could confide without reserve. She introduces her friends, her family history and her own, as well as commenting on the restrictions enforced on Jews by the Nazis during their occupation of Holland.

Margot's summons from the authorities is the spur that hastens their move into hiding, though the Annexe is not yet fully prepared. Their confinement does not produce family harmony, but rather the opposite. The van Daans arrive later to share their hiding place and Anne is far from impressed by them. Little things become irksome in this close association and the two families do not always see eye-to-eye.

They live in constant fear of discovery and start at every noise. They have devised a routine that should prevent anybody in the office or warehouse from suspecting that they are living in the building. The needs of the two families are provided for by Miep, Bep and Mr Kugler.

We are given an intimate insight into Anne's feelings about the others and about herself. The radio brings them the war news; their friends the news of local events. Mr Dussel, the dentist, joins them too and Anne has to share her room with him. He brings stories from the outside world of Jews being persecuted to death. Despite their deprivations, they still manage to celebrate the Jewish festival of Honukkah.

A crisis occurs when the building is sold without their knowledge and only the astuteness of Mr Kleiman averts a potential disaster. They are in constant dread that the warehouse workers, whom they dare not trust, might find that they are hiding there. Local shopkeepers remain sympathetic and ask no questions about where their produce is going.

The families suffer from rats and privation inside and fear of intruders, bombs and anti-aircraft fire from outside. Meanwhile, study courses are taken and Anne becomes distanced from her mother. Anne realises that her sufferings are as nothing compared to those of the Jews outside, but yearns for a more civilised life.

Anne celebrates her first birthday in hiding. Their days are taken up with studying and reading library books. Dussel hinders Anne in her studies and Otto has to intervene. Another break-in and intensified air raids are a cause of concern. Mrs van Daan is rapidly being regarded by Anne as her enemy. Anne describes the daily routine in the Annexe in great detail; the occupants are minutely observed, not always to their advantage. They are all getting on one another's nerves.

Birthdays are still celebrated with presents, but all do not play fair where food is concerned. The families are at a low ebb financially, too, and need to sell possessions to obtain cash.

Bep has to look after her sick sister and Kugler and Kleiman are unable to take her place. This is a serious blow to those in the Annexe, since the purchase of food is now very difficult. Anne, at this time, has disturbing dreams of her friend, Hanneli, and feels remorseful about her previous treatment of her.

Anne feels desperate for someone to confide in; her diary is not enough. She begins to show a more mature approach to her mother. She is filled with wonder at the changes taking place in her own body as she moves towards womanhood and starts to form a relationship with Peter. They find that they are able to talk to each other quite intimately without embarrassment.

Many Dutch people, like those helping the Annexe occupants, are risking their lives in order to help those who are hiding from the Nazis.

The families keep up with the war news through the BBC. Anne now becomes critical of her own behaviour. Her inner loneliness is somewhat alleviated by her meetings with Peter.

Their helpers have troubles of their own and cannot always be available, owing to illness and other obligations. There is concern about the growing relationship between Peter and Anne. When Anne believes Margot to be jealous of this association, she is shown to be mistaken and Margot is depicted in a favourable light. Anne yearns to be free of her parents' shackles and to be independent.

In the Annexe, the adults are obsessed with news bulletins. Outside, the general unrest in the community is reflected in break-ins at the warehouse. The food is monotonous and sparse. Anne continues to hide her real feelings from the adults and keeps her mind occupied with study. Otto speaks with Anne about her relationship with Peter.

Anne distresses her father by giving him a letter in which she expresses her feelings of independence and alienation from her parents. Her father discusses the letter with her and she feels some remorse.

Peter and his parents argue ferociously. Otto's birthday is celebrated by everyone in a generous manner.

Anne feels more in control of her relationship with Peter now. Local news from outside discloses a deterioration of people's attitudes towards the Jews. Their helpers, however, are unwavering in their support, though Miep needs to be reassured by Otto that he believes she is trustworthy.

Bep has become engaged. We are treated to an appraisal of this engagement by Anne, who sees it as a mistake and gives a mature assessment of the situation.

The Franks' funds are running low, but the Allied invasion of France brings them hope of an end to their suffering, though air raids are increasing. Anne analyses both her own situation and the problems faced by the Allies. She also formulates a vision of what the life of a modern woman should be and what rights she ought to have.

Peter has come to depend on Anne; although she is fond of him she is aware that he is not for her. In spite of all that she has been through, she still takes great comfort in the beauty of nature and, like her father, is full of optimism for the future. She is still frustrated at never being able to reveal her inner self, which is so different from her outer self, except to her beloved Kitty.

DETAILED SUMMARIES

PAGES 1–66

PAGES 1–18 BEFORE ENTERING THE ANNEXE

Anne eager to write down her thoughts

Anne's diary is introduced to us as a friend, Kitty. She describes the child-like excitement she experiences in opening her birthday presents, of which her diary is one. She at once gets down to describing her class-mates; we gather that she has admirers.

Inner loneliness

Anne demonstrates humility in thinking that no one would be interested in her writings. The motivation for her writing is her inner loneliness, since she is unable to confide either in friends or family. Her admiration and love of her father come across forcefully in her history of her Jewish family, who have sought refuge in Holland from the Nazis.

Anne was sad to leave her Montessori school and now goes to the Jewish Lyceum, which Margot attends. Her maternal grandmother left Germany to live with them, but died in January 1942. Anne lists all the restrictions that the Germans have forced upon the Jews.

Two of Anne's birthdays passed almost unnoticed, one because of her grandmother's illness and the other because of the war conditions in Holland.

Anne's interest in ping-pong and the resultant trips to the ice-cream parlour give boys an opportunity to show their admiration for her and allow her to manipulate them. At school, she shows a growing maturity in employing humour to win round her maths teacher who is punishing her for her continual chattering.

Lively personality

The obligation to walk everywhere, because transport was denied to Jews, leads to an association with Hello Silberberg, who asks permission to accompany her to school. He is bored by his present girlfriend, Ursula; to him the effervescent Anne is a tonic. Whilst with Hello, Anne is excited by a greeting from Peter Schiff, whom she secretly admires. When Anne and Hello return home ten minutes after curfew, Otto is angry because of his concern for their safety.

Anne's examination results prove satisfactory while Margot's results are excellent as always.

Factories change hands

At this time, Otto has transferred his factories to non-Jews (Opekta to Mr Kleiman and Gies & company to Mr Kugler and Miep and Jan Gies) and is preparing to go into hiding by secreting away clothing, food and furniture and secretly preparing a hideaway.

COMMENT

We have learned a great deal about Anne in these first few pages. There is evidence of the development of a strong personality. She shows a maturity beyond her years and knows how to look after herself, as we can see from her observations of her friends and admirers.

She is cheerful and humorous despite the restrictions Jews have to suffer, and seems oblivious to the preparations for going into hiding. She is obviously an attractive girl with an outgoing personality, concealing an inability to tell others her intimate thoughts. She idolises her father and has a secret yearning for Peter Schiff. This section closes on the sombre note of a move to a life in hiding.

GLOSSARY   **Pogrom** a massacre of Jews, particularly in Russia
              Zionist one dedicated to the establishment of a Jewish state in
              Palestine (now Israel)

PAGES 19–46 THEY GO INTO HIDING

Margot tells Anne that Otto has received a call-up notice (which is in fact for Margot) from the SS, but reassures her that they will avoid it by going into hiding. Their mother has gone to see their friends, the van Daans, who are to go into hiding with them, about it. Otto is away and is unaware of the event. The girls begin to pack and the first item Anne packs is her dairy. Miep and her husband, Jan, take some of the Franks' belongings the evening before the move. They leave the next morning wearing all the clothing they can, since they may not draw attention to their flight by carrying suitcases.

Think about the Franks' choice to go into hiding rather than leaving the country

Their refuge is to be the Annexe, a part of Otto's office building. The office workers, Mr Kugler, Mr Kleiman, Miep Gies and Bep Voskuijl are informed, but the warehousemen know nothing of the plans. A detailed description of the building follows. Because of the urgency of their arrival, the Annexe is unprepared and Anne and her father clear up. Anne becomes overwhelmed with the fear of being discovered. The need for silence is a great burden to Anne, the chatterbox. Miep, Bep and Mr Kleiman are kindly supplying all their requirements.

Anne begins to feel isolated from her mother and Margot, believing that her sister is the favourite. She has a deep affection for her father, however, and realises that part of her problem is to do with her age. She determines to be more realistic in her writing in future.

The van Daans arrive   The Germans are intensifying their campaign against the Jews, as the van Daans arrive at the Annexe. Mr van Daan has told the Franks' former landlord that they have escaped to Belgium and then to Switzerland. This story has received such credence among the neighbours that some people actually 'remembered' happening.

Mr Kugler has the idea of disguising the doorway to their hiding place behind a bookcase, which Bep's father constructs for them.

The van Daan family consists of Mr and Mrs van Daan and Peter, their sixteen-year-old son. Tensions are rising in the confined living space; Anne is not getting on with Mr van Daan or her own mother, nor is she enamoured with Peter, who seems to be a hypochondriac. The two women cannot get along together and further friction arises when Peter surreptitiously reads an 'adult' book, causing dramatic scenes between him and his father.

Anne contents herself with library books and her school work, as best she can. Her interest in royalty is satisfied by listening to Prince Bernhard's broadcasts from London. She is resentful that Margot is allowed to read books which are forbidden to her.

A comic episode in the office is, in Anne's view, an indication of the friendly atmosphere that prevails there, and which is not mirrored in the Annexe. The van Daans want Anne to accept Peter as a brother, but she secretly finds him repulsive at this stage.

Anne criticised
continually

Anne's alienation from her mother and Margot worries her, and she suspects that her mother's demands are not unreasonable. Anne has to put up with a barrage of criticism from Mrs van Daan but Otto defends Anne at times. Mrs van Daan's temperament makes her a figure of fun.

COMMENT   This section opens in an atmosphere of doom. Everybody knew that a call-up notice meant concentration camps and probable death. The esteem in which Otto is held by his erstwhile employees is demonstrated by their willingness to risk their lives daily for him and his family. It is significant that Otto and Anne clear up the Annexe, while Mrs Frank and Margot opt out. They are so afraid that Margot is forbidden even to cough, though she has a cold.

Anne's longing to be treated as an adult and her mother's failure to respond to her wishes plays a major part in their conflicts. We must bear in mind that her mother's view is never heard.

A fine sense of humour is displayed when Anne narrates stories overheard about their mode of departure from home. Anne's commentary on the behaviour of the adults provides evidence of her mature perception; she observes them with an adult eye, while they behave like children. Mrs van Daan's attitude towards Anne is condemned, in the reader's view, by the fair-minded Otto being required to come to his daughter's defence.

PAGES 46–66 DIFFICULTIES OF LIFE IN THE ANNEXE

The washing and toilet facilities in the Annexe and the difficulties they experience when the plumbing fails are described.

The ringing of the doorbell early in the morning frightens them. They also worry that Mr Levinsohn, the chemist who works for Mr Kugler, might want to see the old laboratory which is now the Annexe.

Entertainment

Mrs van Daan foolishly tries to flirt with Otto and Anne reprimands her for it. Peter and Anne amuse them all by dressing up in odd clothes. Bep manages to acquire clothes for Margot and Anne and arranges correspondence courses. Anne shows resentment at being disciplined more strictly than Margot.

Anne is having to make an effort with Edith, though she feels she doesn't love her mother any more. She is now allowed to read more adult books. Otto threatens to take away her diary (she doesn't tell us why) and Anne is terrified that he might. She fantasises about spending money on clothes and make-up.

Nazi persecution

Many of their friends are being arrested by the Gestapo and sent to Westerbork Concentration Camp which is described by an escaped former inmate. From the radio, they learn that Jews are being gassed. Innocent people are being taken hostage by the Gestapo, to be executed whenever any sabotage is committed by the Dutch resistance. This conduct appals Anne and she distances herself from 'those Germans'. Daily studies continue and although Anne loves reading, maths still causes her trouble.

All in the Annexe are worried by noises outside but it is only Mr Kleiman pulling at the bookcase; Miep and her husband stay the night with them and there is some consternation when the lights fuse.

Anne's education continues

Otto becomes ill, but there is no access to medical help. The removal of all her beloved furniture from her home is concealed from Mrs van Daan. Otto is encouraging Anne to read German writers. Her mother gives her a German prayer book.

Tensions persist between Anne and Margot. Anne is expecting her first period. As she reads earlier entries in her diary about puberty, Anne looks upon them with some embarrassment.

Isolation

Anne yearns for physical love and feels isolated. Mr and Mrs Frank appear to see no fault in Margot, much to Anne's annoyance. She is jealous of any affection her father shows to Margot. Anne perceives that she is on the threshold of womanhood.

The news from Stalingrad and North Africa is good, but conditions for Jews in Holland are worsening and they decide to take an extra person into their refuge.

Comment

The families do all they can to have some privacy in the cramped conditions. The terror of discovery is a continual strain on everybody's nerves, yet their spirits are strong and they find ways of having fun.

Anne feels great sadness, both for her own plight and for others. She feels cut off from her mother and Margot at times; it is debatable how much of her irritation is due to puberty and how much to the stresses of their existence.

Study, encouraged by Otto, takes up a good part of the children's day, but Anne does not share her mother's religious bent. She wishes for an unrealistic level of perfection in her parents. There is dramatic irony (see Literary Terms) in her statement that nobody else would ever read her diary. Anne analyses her own writing and aims to improve herself. The families still have consideration for those outside, as we see by their offer to conceal another refugee in their hide-out.

GLOSSARY   **Westerbork** the transit camp for Jews on their way to the gas chambers of Auschwitz
Gestapo Nazi secret police

Identify the speaker.

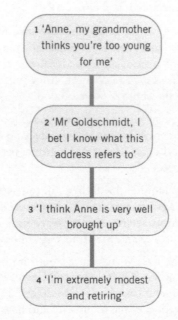

1 'Anne, my grandmother thinks you're too young for me'

2 'Mr Goldschmidt, I bet I know what this address refers to'

3 'I think Anne is very well brought up'

4 'I'm extremely modest and retiring'

Check your answers on page 93.

 Consider these issues.

a What we learn of Anne's character before she entered the Annexe.

b How the Franks get on together before the arrival of the van Daans.

c Anne's attitude towards the Germans and the Dutch.

d Anne's feelings for her mother, her father and Margot in these pages.

e Anne's reappraisal of her previous entries and the statement about her greatest aspiration in life.

f The impression we are given of Mrs van Daan in this section.

PAGES 67–86 THE ARRIVAL OF DUSSEL

Albert Dussel, the dentist, is the man chosen to join them, but he delays his move until he has put his affairs in order. He is amazed that the Franks are not in Belgium. An amusing introductory guide to the Annexe is presented to him. At first, he makes a good impression on Anne, though he brings tragic news of persecution, examples of which Anne has witnessed from her window.

Dussel criticises Anne

Anne finds things to be cheerful about, although she has mood swings and is lonely at times. Electricity has to be rationed. Anne spies on the neighbouring houses. Dussel begins to inform Edith about her daughter's behaviour and lectures Anne. She worries about her character when she is alone in bed at night.

Comic scene

To everyone's delight Mr van Daan makes sausages. Anne depicts the antics of each member of the company, concluding with Mrs van Daan having a tooth pulled. Anne watches the street avidly: passers-by seem generally impoverished and in low spirits, the children neglected. Food is strictly rationed, doubly so in the Annexe.

Mrs van Daan has bruised her ribs and is a difficult patient. Nevertheless, Anne admits that, when well, she is cheerful and hard working. Mr Dussel, however, finds Anne irritating both day and night and continually nags her; she wishes for revenge but, instead, complains to Kitty about the everlasting duty of self-control.

The occupants of the Annexe pass their time filling packets with powdered gravy for Gies & Company. Whatever she does, Anne cannot forget the atrocities that are happening outside. In their hideaway Anne feels they are thinking selfishly.

Anne's nerves are   Anne returns to her own annoyances. Whatever she
frayed   does, she is condemned and is in a frenzy of frustration,
yet she understands it can't always be everyone else's
fault. The others have their own tensions, interspersed
with bouts of humour.

COMMENT   Mr Dussel seems conscientious and inappropriately
fussy, as he delays his escape in order to leave his affairs
in order. The rumour of the Franks' escape to Belgium
has been believed by the neighbours, which may have
dissuaded the authorities from searching for them.

Amidst all their adversity, flashes of humour shine
through and indicate good morale; nor does their
predicament prevent them from feeling for those being
persecuted outside.

Anne's initial good opinion of Mr Dussel does not last
long. He is uninhibited in his criticism of Anne. Nor
does he escape caustic comments from Anne, but only
in her writing. Anne evinces a talent for comic writing:
in the van Daans' kitchen scene, in Peter's mistaken
notice and in the extraction of Mrs van Daan's tooth;
humour relieves the tensions which are arising within
Anne and in the relationships in the Annexe.

The families in the Annexe seek to alleviate their
conditions by the celebration of Hanukkah and
Christmas, complete with presents. This could be
achieved only with the assistance of Bep and Miep,
whose lunch-time visits also help to defuse discord.

We are given an insight into Anne's social conscience
with her concern for the poor she sees outside her
window. Margot has less sympathy. Though Anne is
concerned about her own character, she harbours no
wish to be like Margot, whom everybody else considers
to be the ideal personality. Anne shows a capacity for
introspection and self-analysis, in contrast to her
external displays of confidence and frivolity.

GLOSSARY

Aber but
nicht not
Calisthenics exercises requiring little space or movement
Hanukkah a Jewish festival celebrating the purification of the
   Temple in Jerusalem after it had been defiled by Greeks
menorah a sacred seven-branched candle stick

PAGES 87–121 THE OFFICE BUILDING HAS A NEW OWNER

Fear of discovery The refugees in the Annexe draw some consolation
from the patriotism of the Dutch bishops, but the
sudden arrival in the office of a new landlord brings
them more agitation. Neither Kugler nor Kleiman have
been told that the building has been sold. Kleiman
makes the excuse that he has left the Annexe key at
home and, for the moment, they are safe. They fear,
too, that the warehousemen might betray them. On a
lighter note, Mrs van Daan is given a cheeky nickname.

Food supplies depend upon their ability to pay the
prices charged on the Black Market. Ironically their
potatoes are bought from the German army. The
greengrocer brings his goods when there is no one
about.

Plague of rats Anne is naturally afraid of the air raids, and creeps into
her father's bed for comfort. Burglars are Mrs van
Daan's bugbear. Further disturbance at night is caused
by rats which their cat, Mouschi, deals with.
Nevertheless, Peter is badly bitten by one.

The old currency is being changed and this causes
problems which they overcome by ascribing all monies
to Gies & Company. Another danger in their midst is
Dussel, who has been sending letters to a number of
people, against the rules of the Annexe.

Intruders are heard in the warehouse. Their great fear is
that any police activity, subsequent to a burglary, may

result in the office radio being found tuned in to England. Fortunately, they find no evidence of a break-in. Minor irritations, such as blocked toilets and Mr van Daan's sore throat, pale into insignificance compared to the announcement on the radio of the 'cleansing' of the Dutch provinces of Jews.

Anne's relation-ship with mother at low ebb

Illnesses are affecting their helpers, Kleiman, Bep and her father, Mr Voskuijl. Otto is concerned about the business; he eavesdrops on a meeting with the help of Margot and Anne. There are growing frictions within the families: Edith is distressed when Anne refuses to say her night prayers with her; she feels that her daughter doesn't love her. Anne sees the rebuke in her father's eyes. Everybody else is squabbling, too, and the atmosphere is very poor. Air raids disturb their sleep and their diet is deteriorating.

Dussel behaves childishly about his birthday and receives a food parcel from his partner. They discover that he has secret food supplies which he won't share. Outside, martial law has been declared and rations have been reduced.

Anne longs for a more civilised existence, bewailing the lowering of domestic standards, but she is edified that so many Dutch people are prepared to hide those for whom the Nazis are searching.

Nazi threat to students

The Germans oblige the Dutch university students to show sympathy for the Nazis or be sent to a labour camp. Mrs van Daan is afraid during an air raid and causes hilarity when she goes down to Mr Dussel's bed for comfort.

Otto writes a poem for Anne on her birthday. They hear that Mr Voskuijl has inoperable cancer and cannot help them anymore. Mr Kleiman replaces their radio with a small set when the Germans confiscate all known radios.

Miep a great help   Anne begins to modify her behaviour to keep the peace. Her eyesight has deteriorated but she cannot visit the optician. Miep helps them, shopping daily and bringing them library books each Saturday.

Dussel spiteful   Dussel takes over the table in their room, dismissing Anne's studies as worthless, and spurning her polite request to share it. Only Otto's intervention persuades him to be more reasonable. A real break-in results in the loss of valuables. Heavy raids on Amsterdam continue. There is good news when Mussolini stands down from power. Anne has an argument with Mrs van Daan and Dussel about a book he recommended; she acknowledges that she is still angry. Mr Dussel reacts badly to Kugler's handing over the radio to the authorities. They are plagued by fleas.

COMMENT   The safety of the Annexe depends entirely on others. Their emotions fluctuate between hope and despair.

Anne does not agree with her parents who wish to avoid confrontation, regardless of injustice. Her child's view is shown in her wish that her father should change his production to sweets. Anne is drawn to her father and usually away from her mother as we see during air raids. Otto seems to be the generally accepted leader, as when he stops Dussel's 'letters'.

The fanatical devotion given to Hitler by some of his forces is derided by Anne. She was under no illusions as to what happened to people who were arrested and taken away by the Germans.

Anne justifies her cruel treatment of her mother and seems indifferent to her mother's distress. With Anne, everything seems to be black and white at this stage. Anne is exasperated by her mother, but the whole group are now at loggerheads; the deprivations and close confinement are stretching everybody's nerves.

Dussel's behaviour has sunk to a new low as he hoards food for himself despite what the others have done for him. Anne despises Mr van Daan's pontificating and Mrs van Daan's opinions she dismisses with sharp irony (see Literary Terms). When Anne considers their future, she perceives that their helpers' future and theirs are inextricably linked.

In spite of Anne's contentious behaviour, Otto's affection and understanding are clear from the poem he writes for her birthday. Anne shows gratitude to Mr Voskuijl, whom she considers the greatest source of their safety. The power of radio in boosting the morale of Nazi-occupied Europe is evident from the German campaign to confiscate a radio from every household.

Anne now seems more able to control her behaviour to others, even those she doesn't like. The thought of having to go outside to an optician horrifies Anne. Her annoyance with Dussel seems justified, as can be seen from his pettiness regarding the use of the table; dislike for Anne motivates him since he admits that he would have let Margot use the table. There is more evidence of maturity in Anne than in Dussel. Otto again shows firm leadership in solving the problem.

As they dream about what they look forward to when they are free, all but Otto think of some little pleasure for themselves; he alone is unselfish in wanting to visit Mr Voskuijl.

Anne lists Mrs van Daan's faults after an argument and encapsulates her character in a few lines. Edith, Margot and even Otto do not have much to say in her favour either. Dussel is also increasingly ridiculed.

GLOSSARY   Boche French army slang for 'German': here the name of the
            cat
            Putti Mr van Daan's nickname

Kerli Mrs van Daan's nickname
Pim Otto's nickname
Mussolini Italian dictator during the Second World War

PAGES 121–44 ANNEXE ROUTINE

The Annexe has been their hiding place for a year now and Anne describes their daily routine, beginning with bed-time and bathroom routines which are strictly regulated. During the morning they need to be very quiet, so that the workers do not hear them, but at lunch-time the workers go home and here again the scheme of things is strictly ordered.

Eating habits   Mealtimes allow Anne the opportunity to examine the characters of those present from their approach to food: Mr van Daan is greedy and self-opinionated; Mrs van Daan is also greedy and likes to provoke confrontations; she is hypocritical and bossy. Peter is quiet and never has enough to eat; Margot is also quiet and eats little; her mother eats well and is a good conversationalist; Otto looks after everyone but himself; Anne is described only as 'a little bundle of nerves'; Dussel is the greediest of all and ignores other people's needs; even his toilet habits are described: so regular you can set your watch by them! Bep, who joins them for lunch, enjoys her food and brings a hearty personality to their table.

The Westertoren clock is melted down for the war effort and the families are less sure of the time. Bep has provided new shoes for Anne, of which she is very proud. Anne then has a series of minor injuries which inconvenience her.

Dussel endangers them   Dussel endangers them by sending Miep out for a banned book that could have led to their discovery.

There is a comic scene in which Mrs van Daan tries to engage Dussel and then her husband in futile conversation, managing only to enrage the latter.

The evening routine begins when Bep arrives at 5.30, only to be bombarded with requests by Mrs van Daan. Each then performs his or her appointed task.

Morale in the Annexe has collapsed and people hardly dare speak for fear of provoking an argument. Mr Voskuijl's condition is deteriorating. Hopes are boosted by Italy's surrender, but Mr Kleiman has to go into hospital for a stomach operation. Even valerian fails to lift Anne's depression.

Van Maaren, the warehouseman, is under suspicion for being too inquisitive. Extreme caution is now essential.

Bep being used

Mrs van Daan receives very little for her birthday. Bep is trying to do too much for them and is taken advantage of. Dussel complains that everybody is ignoring him and has to be told why by Edith Frank. The van Daans earn Otto's wrath by cheating over food.

Mr van Daan loses 100 guilders in the warehouse. Workers are suspicious about the money, which is then stolen by an unknown thief.

Clothes must be sold for funds

Mr Kleiman returns and sells some clothes for Mr van Daan. Mrs van Daan claims she has no clothes to spare, but she has a fur coat. Otto is weary of being the Annexe referee. Anne attempts to find relief in study. Even Mr Kleiman's spirits are low, owing to his stomach trouble.

Mrs van Daan's fur coat finally goes for a good price, but she wishes to keep the money for herself. She argues with Mr van Daan before accepting that the money must be used to cover current expenses.

Anne falls into a deep depression. Otto tries to lift their spirits by arranging a correspondence course for Margot and a New Testament project for Anne, the latter a sign of his liberal views as it was considered controversial at the time. Anne's depression has been brought on by fear. She is anxious night and day and feels that normality will never return.

Anne is scolded by everyone for creating dust clouds as she sweeps. Their routine is being relaxed a little, which Anne deems to be careless and dangerous. Only Dussel and the van Daans are trading insults now, as other quarrels recede.

COMMENT   We are given a view of their cramped living conditions and the strict routine.

Anne's attitude towards Mrs van Daan shows itself in the scathing sarcasm she employs to depict her nightly routine. The onomatopoeia (see Literary Terms) of 'creaking' beds and 'sighing' springs brings immediacy to the scene.

Dussel is meticulously observed and we see how primitive their toilet arrangements are. The violence of shooting outside intrudes into the domestic scene.

Anne assesses the characters of the occupants of the Annexe through their approaches to mundane activities (eating, washing, housework). Though various degrees of selfishness are described, Dussel emerges as the greediest and most selfish of all. Bep's presence is an antidote to Dussel's. Mrs van Daan's coy flirting with Dussel and attempts at manipulation of her husband are openly comic. The bravery of Mr Kleiman is noted. Though in a great deal of pain, he never complains and 'the sun begins to shine' when he walks into a room. Bep's generosity is taken advantage of.

The families' routines are Germanic in their consistency. In their situation, simple matters become important. They are disorientated by the removal of the Westertoren clock, as they are unsure of the time; little accidents can cause great difficulties.

Relationships are breaking down in the Annexe. Cash is short and the danger of discovery is increasing. Tantrums and arguments added to fear drive Anne into a deep despair.

GLOSSARY   New Testament section of the Bible concerned with Christ and Christianity

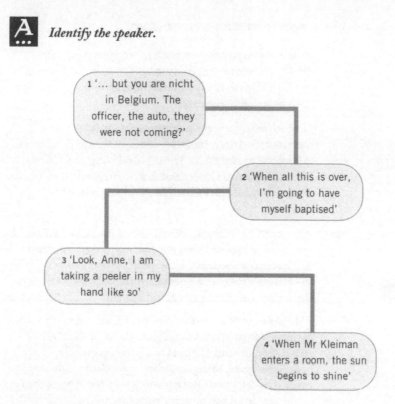

A Identify the speaker.

1 '... but you are nicht in Belgium. The officer, the auto, they were not coming?'

2 'When all this is over, I'm going to have myself baptised'

3 'Look, Anne, I am taking a peeler in my hand like so'

4 'When Mr Kleiman enters a room, the sun begins to shine'

Check your answers on page 93.

B Consider these issues.

a The character of Mr Dussel as revealed in this section.

b The description of Mrs van Daan's dental treatment.

c Anne's feelings for the sufferings of others.

d Anne's introspection and conclusions.

e Anne's refusal to allow her mother to be with her at night prayers.

f The role Otto plays in Anne's life.

g The dangers that break-ins can bring.

Anne inadvertently throws her precious pen, with which she writes her diary, into the stove with some rubbish. She personifies (see Literary Terms) the pen as having been 'cremated'.

The helpers, for various reasons, are unable to continue their services temporarily and the families in hiding feel vulnerable. Dussel is refusing to speak to Mr and Mrs van Daan and Edith attempts to reconcile them. They all agree that Dussel is an absurd character.

Hanneli, a friend in need

One night as Anne is falling asleep, she has a vision of her friend, Hanneli, begging for help. Anne is filled with remorse because, in the past, it must have seemed to Hanneli that Anne became unfriendly. Powerless to help her now, Anne prays for Hanneli.

At Christmas, Otto and Anne produce a poem for each member of the Annexe and put them in their shoes. Anne gets 'flu and Dussel tries, unsuccessfully, to treat her. Anne gives Miep and Bep a fondant made from sugar she has saved. Relationships in the Annexe have improved and a temporary harmony reigns.

Anne considers both the other Jewish children being persecuted and the free people outside. Her spirit is cramped from eighteen months' loss of freedom. She longs to confide in her mother but cannot; as a compromise she begins to call her 'Mums'.

Otto's need

Anne realises that Otto, a bulwark for everybody else, needs to release his own feelings. The helpers take pains to demonstrate their affection by giving them a wonderful Christmas cake.

Again Anne has a vision of Hanneli and of her grandma too. Her affection for her grandmother is clear and Hanneli's suffering teaches Anne that she herself is lucky. All she can do is pray for Hanneli.

Anne criticises Mrs van Daan again and is shocked by the vehement attacks upon her mother written earlier in her diary. She realises that she has treated her mother badly. A new appraisal of her mother is made. Anne has an ideal of what a mother ought to be and is not only dissatisfied in having a mother as merely a friend, but is also hurt that her mother laughs at her tantrums.

Anne views with wonder the changes that are taking place in her body as she reaches puberty. She is growing up fast and feels an immense need for a female companion. Peter will have to do instead.

Anne visits Peter's room

She does not want to be a nuisance to Peter, but finds that helping him with his crosswords is a good excuse to prolong visits to his room. She finds it humiliating to have to ask for companionship. The Peter she dreams of, however, is Peter Schiff. Anne reminisces about her time with Peter Schiff, who was older than she was and finally left her for other girls. Anne's classmates found her attractive, but none made her feel like Peter Schiff.

The latest of Anne's crazes is ballet. She dresses the part and practises daily. She is also interested in the genealogy of royal families and collecting pictures of film stars. Her mother is reading a book about the problems of adolescents, but Anne thinks she should take more interest in the real thing. Her relationship with Margot is improving.

Even before going into hiding, Anne felt an estrangement from her family and an essential loneliness. She consoles herself that she now has her beloved 'Peter' to help her.

Mrs van Daan is jealous of Edith's birthday present from Mr Kugler. Anne feels guilty about her own

Anne more
objective

self-centredness, and tries to forgive her mother. She can see even Mrs van Daan in a more objective light and attributes this new way of seeing others to her dream of Peter Schiff. She determines to be more mature and to give up chattering.

Anne's sex education has come partly from her father and partly from friends. Discussions on sex were either sordid or embarrassing. To Anne's surprise, she and Peter talk about sex naturally and without embarrassment.

At table, there is a dearth of good conversation and people tell the same stories repeatedly. They even repeat and embellish others' stories.

Bravery of the
Dutch

There are many resistance groups in Holland helping out those in hiding. Their own helpers also risk their lives to help. The Dutch authorities, where they can, actively assist those in hiding; ration books are issued illegally and there is even a football match between the Military Police and those who had gone underground.

Anne is desperate to be alone, but cannot be. The families make plans about what to do if the Allies reach Amsterdam. Invasion is the daily topic. Their supplies of food appear to be sufficient. They know they can rely on the truth of the BBC news bulletins. Anne has become fatalistic about it all.

COMMENT

Anne **personifies** (see Literary Terms) her pen as she does her diary, because it is of special value to her and she treats it with great care.

Anne's views of Mrs van Daan and Mr Dussel illustrate her maturity of thought, which is not always translated into practice. The vividness of her imagination is sharply expressed through the description of her dreams and 'visions' and her concern through her prayers for

Hanneli. She has mood swings due to the situation and her age.

Anne's loneliness is plain from her distress when she feels misunderstood by her mother 'every day and every hour of the day' and yearns to be free to behave like any normal teenager.

Anne shows signs of growing more mature now, as the previous diary entries about her mother appal her and she aims for a more balanced approach. Her self-pity had blinded her to the effect of her behaviour on those around her. The example she gives of not being allowed to accompany Margot and her mother into town because she had her bike with her is an example of how childish her behaviour is at times. It is hardly surprising that Margot and her mother sometimes laughed at her. Other examples suggest that Anne was also justified in her feelings at times (the incident over the pin in Margot's blanket, for example).

Though her emotions are volatile, she looks upon her development with awe and delight. As her body develops, she feels she is becoming independent, but she has a deep need for a close companion. Day-dreaming about Peter Schiff is an attempt to satisfy that need.

Anne has the ability to stand back and analyse her faults. She finds some relief for her loneliness in Peter van Daan, in whom she can, to some degree, confide.

GLOSSARY   figuratively not literally
                      Petel Peter Schiff

Pages 185 –211 **PETER AND ANNE BEGIN A RELATIONSHIP**

Anne notices that Peter van Daan is looking at her in a strange way which makes her feel good. An altercation between Dussel and Peter allows Peter the opportunity to talk to Anne. He admires her way with words, which he lacks, and is relieved that he can confide in her.

Dussel falsely claims that Peter has apologised to him. This causes a further row when Peter finds out. Peter looks for occasions to talk to Anne. He pays her compliments, not in words but with his eyes. Peter has aspirations to live on a rubber plantation in the Dutch East Indies when the war is over. Anne is sad that he intends to hide his Jewishness. Their conversation is wide-ranging as well as personal. Anne realises that Peter, too, is in need of affection, though his feelings of inferiority cause her some irritation.

Edith objects to visits to Peter's room

Peter wants Anne to come to his room and read her stories to him as she does to his mother. This new closeness to Peter has transformed her days, but her mother objects to her visits to Peter's room, thus engendering Anne's hatred and distress. Anne doubts Peter's feelings towards her when she is melancholy.

They have a strict routine on Sunday in the Annexe. Anne relates the procedures in detail. Whatever Mr Dussel does is annoying.

Anne and Peter share a closeness that does not require speech, as they contemplate the scene through the window; Anne finds peace and hope in observing nature and in Peter's company. Peter has become an obsession with her now. They both hide their true feelings from others, Peter by withdrawing into himself and Anne by being boisterous. Anne's awakening sexuality fuses the two Peters in her life into one. She is desperate to hide from the others the yearning and frustration that overwhelms her.

Another break-in has occurred, the circumstances of which suggest that someone might possess a key. They fear it could be one of the warehousemen, who might betray them.

Bep needs support   Bep is becoming disconsolate and Anne longs to comfort her, but is not allowed to. She is frustrated by the attitude of the adults who will not hear her opinions and feels that the older members ought to provide for the younger the love they crave. Anne finds Mrs van Daan more approachable than her own mother, which upsets Edith.

Anne and Peter discuss their parents' failings. Peter admires Otto. Anne advises him to talk with her father. Peter is overwhelmed to learn that Otto has a good opinion of him.

Anne finds consolation in her belief that her Grandma is looking after her, and in her close association with Peter which, she feels, is bordering on love. His shy, retiring manner makes her hesitate to trust that he feels the same. Nevertheless, he has lifted her spirits. They are alone together so much that Mrs van Daan jokingly wonders whether they can be trusted. Anne feels she must protect Peter from being misjudged and empathises with his loneliness and need for affection. Anne knows they can help each other if only he will allow it.

Self-analysis by   In looking back on her previous life, Anne concludes
Anne   that she has been spoiled by her parents, friends and admirers. Her attributes she considers superficial. Forgoing all the admiration has been difficult but has made her grow up. She now requires friends who respect her for who she is, not for her external personality. She sees her future intertwined with Peter's and her thoughts are more positive. She is grateful to God for all she has and believes 'a person who has courage and faith will never die in misery'.

COMMENT   Peter and Anne are drawn together by their mutual
           isolation, loneliness and adolescence, which the adults
           do not understand. Though very different people on the
           outside, they both struggle to conceal their feelings
           from others and need someone to confide in. Anne
           cannot get Peter out of her mind, but we are not party
           to Peter's thoughts of her. In Anne's eyes, this most
           precious friendship is opposed by her mother, which
           makes her very unhappy. Neither of their mothers
           supports them and Anne longs to help Peter. Otto is
           the only one among the adults who is held by the
           young ones to be blameless.

           The Annexe routine operates even on Sunday when no
           one is in the warehouse or office, as if it provides a kind
           of security. Bep's boyfriend has been taken away to
           Germany.

           Anne's spirituality is evident here: she equates God
           with the beauties of nature; she feels her grandmother's
           presence protecting her and believes that faith and
           courage can avert a miserable death; she prays. Anne
           has matured considerably since she went into hiding
           and sees her previous attitude to life as shallow. She
           looks for deeper attachments now. Her erratic
           behaviour is explained as an effort to try to balance
           things after her cosy world has fallen apart. The sad
           truth is that she has given up on any relationship with
           her mother, could not confide in her father and has to
           rely on her own resources.

GLOSSARY   Mouschi a cat
           rambunctious boisterous

PAGES 211–45 HELPER ARRESTED

           Matters are taking a turn for the worse as one of their
           helpers, identified only as Mr M, is arrested, Miep and

Mr Kleiman are ill and Bep, alone, is left to support them. They take fright at someone knocking on their wall at night, but nothing comes of it. Anne is consoled by her visits to Peter, which they both enjoy, and she is extremely inquisitive about him and fears that his feelings towards her have changed. She puts on a brave face, refusing to allow Margot into her confidence, though she would like to help.

Their food supply is threatened when those who provide them with food coupons are arrested. Their diet consequently deteriorates and the Annexe reeks of bad food.

Mrs van Daan is full of self-pity and pessimism about the war, while Otto is optimistic and thinks of sharing what he has with Bep.

Illness strikes helpers

Bep, Miep and Kleiman are still unwell and Mr Kugler has received call-up papers to a compulsory work unit. Only Jan Gies can visit them briefly each day. He tells them how medical care is deteriorating due to a lack of doctors.

Anne has no privacy. Her moods are isolating her from all members of her family, but she maintains a brave exterior, even with Peter. Their fears of an end to their food supplies are eased, as Bep recovers and Mr Kugler escapes the work duty.

Both girls need more freedom

Margot and Anne feel they are under constant observation and treated as children despite their increasing maturity. Anne is less affectionate to her parents.

Anne is bemused by parents being unable to talk to their children about sex. She has had to work out the mechanics of sex for herself and has had her ideas clarified by her friend, Jacque, and by Peter.

Anne is reduced to tears when Peter refuses her offer of food, because she mistakenly assumes he is angry with her. A reconciliation takes place in his room, where they indulge in a heart-to-heart conversation, in which they discuss the frustration they feel with their parents. The male and female responses are very different: Anne goes to bed and weeps while Peter goes up to his room and swears. Anne is surprised that she cheers Peter up. They have both reversed their earlier opinions of each other. Anne is overwhelmed with joy at the closeness of their relationship.

Anne has to restrict her visits to Peter in order to appease her parents and to avoid hurting Margot who, she mistakenly feels, likes Peter. Neither of her parents is pleased with Anne's behaviour at this point.

Margot and Anne
exchange letters

Because the opportunity to talk privately is very limited, Margot and Anne have taken to writing to each other. Both girls share similar needs, but Margot is not jealous about Peter and is happy for them to be close. Another reason Anne writes to Margot is because she finds it easier to express her thoughts that way and she tells of the respect she has for Margot.

Peter and Anne
growing closer

For her part, Margot thinks of Peter as a younger brother. Anne's friendship with him is developing into something more. Peter is very welcoming to her and obviously enjoys her company.

A certain restlessness in Peter one night disturbs Anne, making her feel that something is wrong. In a note to Margot, Anne invites her to join them.

The food 'coupon' men are released and Miep returns. Once more they are terrified by explosions and gun fire as an Allied plane is brought down close by.

Peter and Anne engage in an intimate discussion about sex and contraception, about which Peter is very knowledgeable. Overhearing the two girls speaking in the bathroom later, Peter thinks they are ridiculing him and confronts Anne. Anne, mortified, has to assure Peter that she is able to keep confidences.

Peter and Anne are becoming the butts of jocular remarks from the adults. Edith is, not unnaturally, eager to know what they talk about but doesn't dare ask. Anne understands how shocked their parents would be if they knew the intimacy of their conversations. Anne describes female genitalia to Kitty as though she has just acquired the knowledge herself.

Anne more sure of herself

Anne feels that she has grown up considerably while in the Annexe. She can now view matters with more objectivity, she believes, instead of accepting only her parents' opinions. She has discovered how to influence Mr and Mrs van Daan. Anne wins her father's support for her visits to Peter. She regards her strongest assets to be her optimistic nature and love of people.

In their isolation, they hear many dubious rumours, but they trust the BBC news broadcasts.

Anne fuels arguments about the war with enjoyment. They are not deceived by the propaganda broadcast by the German radio. Anne is amazed that the adults can listen to the news hour after hour and she depicts a scene as they all gather round the radio, only to begin another argument when the broadcast finishes.

Otto defends Anne

According to Anne, Mrs van Daan is jealous of her visits to Peter's room and Edith would rather her daughter didn't go, but Otto tells Anne she doesn't have to take notice of Mrs van Daan. Mrs Frank thinks that Peter is in love with Anne. Anne wishes this were so, since she seems to be in love with him.

A Dutch politician in England requests that his countrymen keep diaries about the conditions they are suffering in war time, so that they can be published after the war. Anne dreams of publishing her novel, 'The Secret Annexe'.

Anne acknowledges that she has not told the whole story: the terrible air raids; the disease, the breakdown of public morality; the lack of food; the slave labour; the many acts of sabotage; but, on a happier note, informs us that very few Dutch people are on the German side.

Anne is calmed by her friendship with Peter but she is unnerved by being uncertain whether Peter sees her as a friend or a loved one, as she yearns for greater intimacy.

COMMENT   The arrests of Mr 'M', who has been supplying them with food, and of the other Black Marketeers indicates the risks taken by the local population and the oppression which is all around them.

Though meeting Peter is the highlight of Anne's day, tension arises from her inability to decipher his attitude towards her. Anne's reactions are often extravagant.

Margot does not feature in the diary as much as we might expect, but when she does she is mainly seen in a good light, as she is here, wanting to help Anne with her problems.

The members of the Annexe react to the privations differently, according to their character. The essential importance to them of their helpers is evident when there is the threat of withdrawal.

Society appears to be falling apart as medical services crumble and public morality deteriorates.

While Anne undergoes all the extremes of emotion in her feelings for Peter, she is also embattled with her mother, to whom she now feels superior, resenting any restraint which Edith might impose on her. Anne feels imprisoned by the unending surveillance of her parents, from which she strives to be free. Her ideal of motherhood has been conjured up from her own needs.

Anne is moving closer to Margot and the device of writing notes to each other allows them to speak intimately and privately whilst surrounded by people. Though they are different in temperament, Anne and Peter share similar problems and conceal their real thoughts from the adults. Their intimate conversations about sex bind them closer in a shared secret. Peter misinterprets Anne's mother's interest in what they talk about in his room; Mrs Frank is justly concerned for her daughter's well being and it may have little to do with jealousy.

We again have to admire the understanding and trust which Otto exhibits for his daughter. Though Anne feels she is growing more mature, she manifests little conception of the possible validity of her mother's concern for her. Where once she could manipulate young admirers, she finds she can now manipulate adults.

GLOSSARY   prophylactic   contraceptive

propaganda   news designed to persuade to a specific point of view

PAGES 246–77   FOOD CYCLES

There is a shortage of food throughout Holland, not just in the Annexe, where the result is that their diet becomes bland and repetitive. Anne takes it all in her stride.

Anne oscillates in her attitude to schoolwork. She is in a depression in which the effort of hiding her feelings and appearing cheerful to others is translated into fits of sobbing when alone. Even the comfort of her friendship with Peter is dimmed.

Anne realises the value of study

She decides she must study in order to achieve her journalistic ambition. She gets great pleasure from writing stories and knows the strengths and weaknesses of the two stories she has written (Eva's Dream and Cady's Life). Se wants to touch many people's lives and 'go on living even after my death' but she is aware of the limitations of her youth.

Anne lists her hobbies as: writing, genealogy, history, Greek and Roman mythology, reading, film stars, with history as her favourite; music moves her deeply and she hates mathematics.

Anne takes the only cushion in her room into the attic to sit on while talking to Peter. Dussel creates a commotion because he fears it might become infested with fleas. Peter and Anne respond mischievously.

Terror of discovery after break-in

Another break-in disturbs them and although they frighten the burglars away, others come to investigate the noise. Their terror affects their bowels and they have to use a metal paper basket for a toilet. Mrs van Daan wants to hide the radio in case the police return and proposes to burn Anne's diary, but Anne will have none of it and tries to imbue Mrs van Daan with some courage. They decide to telephone Mr Kleiman the next day. Miep and Jan Gies arrive.

Peter the bravest

The nightwatchman has searched the building with one policeman. The police plan to continue their investigations the following day. It transpires that the man who investigated the noise is a friend, Mr van Hoeven, who supplies their greengrocery. During a subsequent air raid, Peter and Anne cuddle each other for comfort and, in Anne's eyes, he is the bravest of them all. Amidst their fear, they still had thought for those who were helping them.

A stricter regime is put into operation. They do not know whether the nightwatchman can be trusted. Anne attributes their burdens to God, who will also raise them up again to a better future. She tells of her love of the Dutch and her desire to become a Dutch citizen.

Anne has confidence in her own strong spirit and is full of the ideals of youth, comparing herself favourably to her mother.

Everybody's nerves are on edge and minor plumbing problems arise, but spring is in the air outside and Anne reflects on the contrast with the miserable atmosphere in the Annexe.

Carelessness brings danger Mr Kugler is furious at having to break into the building because Peter forgot to unbolt the front door. He is angry that the people next door have seen the Annexe windows open, too. Peter is dismayed at his carelessness and Anne wishes to console him.

The plumbing problems in the Annexe are remedied, but diet is still poor. The war news from abroad is mixed; the only hope for Holland is an Allied invasion.

Peter & Anne kiss Anne is overwhelmed with joy when, after an evening with their arms around each other, Peter kisses her. She makes the conditions of the time the excuse for their behaviour but feels guilty and decides to mention it to her father. She wants matters to progress.

Anne teaches Peter about the female body, which ends in a second kiss. She feels the need for more intimacy and wishes to enjoy the burgeoning spring with Peter forever undisturbed.

Van Maaren infuriates Bep by accusing her of stealing flour. Anne thinks he is the thief. Even in hiding, they manage to have furniture valued and Anne plans to try to have one of her fairy tales printed.

Dussel a danger   Dussel sulks about the new security measures. He defies
                      the rules and is confronted first by van Daan and then
                      by Otto, whom he insults. Mr Voskuijl is dying of
                      cancer. Anne tries out her new story on her family with
                      some success.

                      Mrs van Daan does nothing but grumble now. Anne
                      studies intensely during the day. Her infatuation with
                      Peter Schiff in her imagination finds its living parallel
                      in Peter van Daan. Anne is overcome with emotion at
                      being with him and is in tears. The strength of her
                      emotion after their first real kiss frightens her and she
                      has difficulty behaving normally with the others after
                      she leaves Peter. She recognises that Peter is not for her
                      permanently, but the power of her sexual awakening
                      scares her. Peter agrees that she should speak to her
                      father.

Otto's advice   Otto does not condemn Anne but gives her a gentle
                      warning that the onus is on her to show restraint and
                      that she should not take the relationship too seriously.
                      He later speaks to Peter about the matter. Anne
                      wonders whether Peter will bother about her when they
                      are free. Though Otto wants Anne to reduce her visits
                      to Peter, she resolves to disobey him.

COMMENT   Anne puts up with her situation without complaint.
                      She puts on a brave act, even to Peter, until she is in
                      the privacy of her own bed. She is a spirited girl whose
                      consolation and ambition lie in writing.

                      One weakness of Anne's is her inability to understand
                      other people's viewpoints when they affect herself;
                      Dussel is castigated for complaining about her taking
                      his cushion but his point about the fleas is not
                      unreasonable.

                      The scene about the intruders is dramatically dealt with
                      and the fear experienced is graphically portrayed. A

moment of tension when it is suggested that Anne's diary be burnt demonstrates how close we were to losing this work altogether. Only Anne's determination saved it. Otto's authority within the group is evident from the fact that he ensured that the diary was safe. During the air raid, it is noticeable that Anne now prefers the company of Peter ('the bravest of them all') to her father's.

The families now have another person, the nightwatchman Sleegers, whom they do not know if they can trust.

Anne sees herself and her fellow sufferers as a part of the great history of the Jews, persecuted yet surviving for some divine purpose. She is aware of and confident about her own ability and knows she can do better in life than her mother.

There appears to be no problem getting men into the Annexe to do repairs. The only explanation as to how this is done is 'Thanks to our many connections'. Their contact with the outside (workmen, valuations) shows that they had to trust their lives to strangers, presumably on the word of their helpers. We can appreciate Mr Kugler's frustration when his life is endangered by the carelessness of the people in the Annexe.

In the arms of Peter with spring in the air, Anne can find no sympathy for the others with their 'grumpy faces'. As Anne's friendship with Peter becomes more intimate, her heart rules her head as she dismisses the adults' concern, though her own doubts are evident in all the rhetorical questions she asks herself within the space of a few lines. Peter van Daan has now reached the status of the Peter Schiff of Anne's dreams. It is to Peter's credit that he agrees that Anne should tell her father. Otto's paternal care and guidance show themselves in his speaking to both of them about their friendship. The strength of her passion is greater than her duty of obedience to her father.

GLOSSARY   endive a kind of chicory

Nazi a member of Hitler's National Socialist Party

Fuhrer leader, a title applied to Hitler

A *Identify the speaker.*

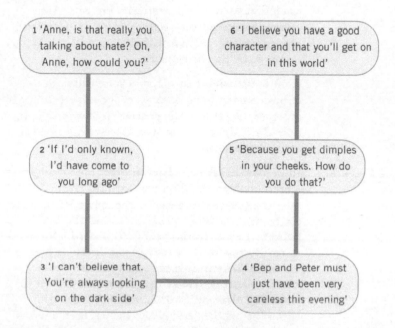

1 'Anne, is that really you talking about hate? Oh, Anne, how could you?'

6 'I believe you have a good character and that you'll get on in this world'

2 'If I'd only known, I'd have come to you long ago'

5 'Because you get dimples in your cheeks. How do you do that?'

3 'I can't believe that. You're always looking on the dark side'

4 'Bep and Peter must just have been very careless this evening'

Check your answers on page 93.

 B *Consider these issues.*

a The behaviour of Dussel.

b Anne's reappraisal of her mother.

c Anne's need for a special friend.

d Anne's romantic dreams.

e The relationship between Peter and Anne.

f How Margot's character is disclosed in this section.

g The terror of the break-in.

h The part Otto plays in the Anne-Peter relationship.

Dussel apologises to Mr van Daan for upsetting him, just in time to receive his birthday presents. Anne believes that an invasion in the West of Holland will happen. Outside, high inflation means a Black Market boom; wages have been frozen.

Anne understands that human nature will need to change in order to be rid of war. She sees her future life differing from that of the generation of women at the time. She analyses her assets and feels exhilarated at becoming a woman.

Anne proclaims her independence

Anne gives her father a letter in which she claims the right to live her own life as an adult, without interference from her parents. She upbraids him and her mother for failing to help her when she was unhappy and for reprimanding her instead. Otto is extremely upset by the letter; Anne dismisses his reaction as oversensitive, but when he sees Anne about her letter he refutes her accusation of their not caring. Anne will withdraw nothing she said against her mother, but knows she has been unfair to

Otto shows Anne another perspective

her father. She is full of remorse for what she has done. We learn that Otto had made an attempt at suicide.

Anne relates her family history. Her father is from a wealthy family whose riches were lost through hyper-inflation. Her mother's family were comfortably off, but the Franks are not overly rich now. Anne's ambitions are to travel and learn languages, whereas Margot wants to nurse new-born babies.

Miep regales them with mouth-watering accounts of a party, where she noted the names of two police officers present, in case they could be of service later.

Anne has finished her fairy story and made it into a little book to give to her father for his birthday. Margot and Edith write poems for him.

A new office worker unwittingly curtails their afternoon activities and Mr Dussel's toilet habits are pinned to the toilet door by Anne while he is inside.

Dramatic haircut

In preparing to cut Peter's hair, his mother and Peter argue violently. After Peter's sham of an apology, Mr van Daan berates him for his behaviour. The van Daan squabbles amuse and concern the others by turns.

The public library provides all the books for Anne's wide-ranging studies. Her wish is to become a famous writer and she has plans to publish her diary. Her story 'Cady's Life' has its basis in her own father's life. Mr Frank receives good presents for his birthday and reciprocates the generosity shown him. Anne enumerates the various interests of the occupants of the Annexe.

Anne is more in control of herself now in her relationship with Peter. She no longer reveals to him her innermost feelings. All Anne's work is soaked and her melodramatic reaction has all the family laughing at her.

Anti-Jewish feeling

All talk now is of the impending invasion and bets are being laid as to the date. They are all saddened by news of a rise in anti-Jewish feeling in Holland. Anne thinks it sad that the enemies of the Nazis are being corrupted by the views they are fighting against.

Bep Voskuijl becomes engaged to Bertus. Anne is against the marriage because Bep does not love him.

Mr van Hoeven, the man who brought them greengrocery, has been arrested for harbouring Jews. They will have less to eat since Bep cannot carry the heavy bags he used to bring.

COMMENT   Dussel's insincerity is exposed as he ends a quarrel easily when it serves to his advantage. The consideration shown to the families in the Annexe is not restricted to feeding them: Mr Kleiman is willing to get anything which will make their lives more comfortable. Miep's caring attitude is highlighted by her noting the names of the police officers she meets; at every turn, she is scheming how to assist those in hiding. The efficient determination of the Nazis in the conduct of their persecution of Jews and others and the consequent danger which their helpers expose themselves to is clear.

Anne's youthful optimism continues despite the hardship, uncertainty and fear for herself and for society. Her feelings for Peter are less overwhelming. Even when Peter betrays a violent streak towards his mother, it fails to alter Anne's opinion of him. Her impetuous letter to her father reveals the arrogance and self-importance of adolescence. Her claims to maturity are undermined by her assumption that anyone who does not accept her verdict is wrong. To her credit, Anne acknowledges her self-righteousness and she is filled with remorse after her talk with Otto. Otto, once again, proves his nobility of character, understanding and care by treating Anne with great kindness afterwards.

Anne's story of 'Cady's Life', based on Otto's life, would seem to imply that Otto married 'second best', though we have no corroboration of this from any other source. Otto's kindness surfaces again here when he presents gifts to the others on his birthday. The presents he receives from Kugler, Dussel, the van Daans, Miep and Bep are a measure of their affection for him.

The petty squabbles between Mr and Mrs van Daan are trivial not just in Anne's imagination, but in reality, as we can see verbatim how one of them develops. The people hiding in the Annexe are unusual in the breadth of their interests, as their studies reveal.

Anne is capable of rational and objective thought as we can gather from her analysis of Britain's conducting of the war and also in the way Jews are all condemned by the behaviour of one, whereas each Christian is not considered to represent all Christians. Her consideration of Bep's forthcoming marriage is a mature assessment too.

GLOSSARY   the Great War   the First World War (1914–18)

PAGES 303 –34   **THE STRESS OF THEIR SITUATION**

Emotions are volatile in the Annexe; they live their lives in a kind of hysteria. Their helpers are given credit; Mr Kugler's responsibilities are causing him unbearable stress. Bep and Mr Kleiman find some release in outside activities. Those in the Annexe find none.

Worried by arrests   Problems with plumbing again arise and the arrest of van Hoeven has shaken them badly. Miep is very concerned that those in the Annexe might think that their helpers could be swayed by the current wave of anti-Semitism. Otto's protestations do not entirely convince Miep. Anne pays respect to their nobility of spirit, while she is at the end of her tether and wants it all to finish one way or another.

Hot weather makes the Annexe uncomfortable because they must not open the windows. Dussel and the Franks have a confrontation in which Dussel is the loser. He is becoming too familiar with Mrs van Daan. Petty jealousies are causing an evil atmosphere. Their funds are so low that they will not last the month.

They are sceptical when the invasion of France is
announced, but when they become convinced, their
spirits are lifted. Mrs van Daan now has to change the
subject of her complaints, but still complains.

On her fifteenth birthday, the last she was ever to
celebrate, Anne receives plenty of presents but seems
disappointed with Peter's present. The Dutch people
appear to believe that the British will occupy Holland;
Anne seems to believe it not unreasonable that they
will.

Anne compares
herself to the
adults

Anne feels superior intellectually to Dussel and Mrs van
Daan. Her complainants see their own defects in her
and it is possible the reverse might also be true. When
Mrs Frank joins in, Anne thinks that no one
understands her and she longs for someone to do so.
She no longer views Peter as the 'real thing'.

Anne is a thoroughly modern young woman, who feels
deeply the injustices that women have been subjected to
and makes a plea for full equality of the sexes.

Mrs van Daan's nerves are deteriorating, yet she
receives no sympathy from Anne. Anne believes in self-
preservation at this stage. Potatoes are in short supply
and each is given a ration to use as they wish. Bep is
suffering from depression, Kleiman may have an
operation and Miep is taking a break. News of the war
is good.

Dussel the dentist

Anne is having painful dentistry from Mr Dussel and
Mrs van Daan develops toothache too. Peter and
Margot wish they had Anne's drive and courage. Anne
is unhappy at Peter's dependence on her and is
concerned to help him to help himself, but they hold
completely contrasting attitudes to life.

The arrival of a large consignment of strawberries
results in a frenzy of consuming and preserving which is

interrupted by visits from the postman and the accountant. The next job is preparing peas. The monotony of the task sets Anne off chattering about anything that enters her head to general amusement. Her wish never to be a housewife is confirmed.

Anne's self-analysis

Anne gives an account of her character. She claims to know herself well, having an ability to observe her actions with detachment. She believes it is up to her to improve her character and behaviour. She is a private person who resents adult advice and wants to sort things out for herself. Anne surmises that life in the Annexe is easier for the adults than the children. She understands that ideals are, in practice, unattainable, but remains optimistic about human nature. She draws comfort from nature, which she imagines will cure all present evils in time.

An attempt on Hitler's life fails and he places all military personnel under the authority of the Gestapo. Anne anticipates a return to school in October.

The two Annes

Anne sees herself as a 'bundle of contradictions'. Outwardly, she is self-opinionated, volatile, cheerful, optimistic. Inwardly, she is quiet, serious and deeply thoughtful. She attributes other people's dislike of her to the fact that her actions do not respond to the dictates of her inner self. If she behaves in a serious manner, her family think she is ill or sulking, which leaves her in a state of constant frustration at not being allowed to portray her real self, which she finds it difficult to do anyway. This is how the last entry in her diary concludes.

COMMENT

We are made aware of the immense strain the helpers add to their private concerns by supporting the Annexe families.

Anne's soul-searching is very moving. She does not need others to recite her faults to her; in this she shows more maturity than they. When her mother criticises her, Anne has some justification in saying Edith does not understand her.

Anne has been able to dissociate herself so completely from her German origin that she always speaks of Germans as though they are foreigners to her and she rejoices in their downfall.

Anne needs Peter to share his innermost feelings before she can reciprocate and his inability to do so frustrates her need to confide in someone without any restraint. The reader can easily see that Peter and Anne are not really suited to each other, but have just been thrown together by circumstance. She is strong-willed, forceful and energetic, whereas he has no positive thoughts for his future. The last thing Anne needs is for someone to be utterly dependent on her, though she does want to help him.

Anne is a creative person and mundane monotonous tasks frustrate her, furthering her ambition to escape from household chores. She observes her actions from an objective standpoint, believing it is her responsibility to improve herself. Like her father, she herself is a private person and perhaps could not open up entirely to anybody.

When she agrees that 'Deep down the young are lonelier than the old' she does not understand the meaning of the word 'old' in this context and relates it to the adults in the Annexe, although they are not old within the meaning of the quotation. In stressful times like theirs, the adults bore more responsibility than Anne, in her youth, could imagine.

Her buoyant idealism can never be annihilated; it is part of her optimistic nature. She feels a sense of doom and yet looking at nature brings her hope.

Her analysis of herself depicts a struggle between two
natures, the external and the internal, and she longs to
express her inner self, rejecting the image she has
projected all her life. She does not realise that the face
she shows the world is an essential part of her nature,
too, and makes her into the fascinating and attractive
person she is.

GLOSSARY   Sodom and Gomorrah biblical cities destroyed for their sins
             Whitsun Pentecost, the birthday of the Christian Church
             D-Day the day the Allies invaded German-occupied France
             Bolsheviks Russian Communists
             purgatory in Christian teaching, a place where souls undergo a
              process of purification before entering heaven
             hulling taking off strawberry stalks
             Allies the countries in alliance against Hitler

A *Identify the speaker.*

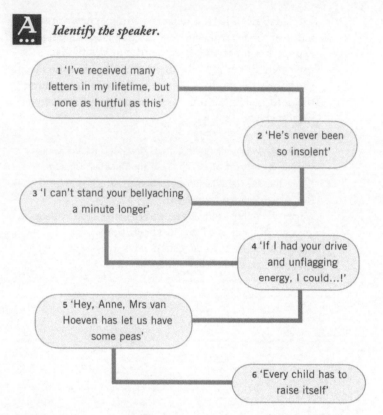

1 'I've received many letters in my lifetime, but none as hurtful as this'

2 'He's never been so insolent'

3 'I can't stand your bellyaching a minute longer'

4 'If I had your drive and unflagging energy, I could...!'

5 'Hey, Anne, Mrs van Hoeven has let us have some peas'

6 'Every child has to raise itself'

Check your answers on page 93.

B *Consider these issues.*

a Anne's description of herself.

b The letter which Anne gives to her father.

c Otto's view of things.

d Mrs van Daan's attempt to cut Peter's hair.

e Anne's story based on her father's life.

f The stage reached in Anne and Peter's romance.

g Mr van Hoeven's arrest and its consequences.

h Anne's views on women's emancipation.

PART THREE

COMMENTARY

THEMES

ADOLESENCE

The entire book is composed of the views and feelings of a teenage girl about herself, the people with whom she comes into contact and the world outside. Three adolescents occupy the Annexe and teenage issues permeate the diary.

Initially Anne is a confident teenager full of fun, with plenty of friends and admirers.

Much of her behaviour is typically adolescent: Anne experiences frustration and indignation at restrictions imposed on her as a child, while she is becoming an adult; much of her frustration is vented on her mother. She is also very sensitive to criticism and feels quite alone in the world. It is her loneliness, sexual awakening and innocence, and her romantic imagination that attract her to Peter and cloud her judgement.

Anne possesses a youthful idealism; she cares intensely about those who are suffering outside, but is less able to care for those with whom she lives.

Anne champions equality of the sexes and aims to be a woman who is creative and works outside the domestic environment. She is a teenager looking towards a reformed world.

Anne matures during the course of the diary, becoming clearer about her own faults and strengths, and being more understanding of others.

Peter is a self-consciousness and awkward adolescent. He, like Anne, experiences a deep loneliness and need of love which he covers up with bravado. He has no wish to confide in his parents as they would like him to, and can be rebellious.

Margot shows a lack of physical energy, not unknown in adolescent girls. She also experiences loneliness and the need to be loved. She, too, is annoyed by being too closely observed by her parents and needs more freedom.

The three teenagers have to endure the highs and lows of adolescence in unusually isolated circumstances, without the support and stimulation of their contemporaries or society at large.

TYRANNY AND REPRESSION

The effects of the Nazi persecution of the Jews appear first in Anne's statement that the Franks emigrated to Holland because they were Jewish. This is quickly followed by a reference to Hitler's anti-Jewish laws and the pogroms.

Anne lists the restrictions imposed on the Jews after the German conquest of Holland, designed to control their movements and divide them from the rest of society. Repression comes at this time entirely from the Germans.

The Nazi authorities burst into their lives with the call-up notice delivered upon Margot and the terror of being arrested persists through to the tragic end. The diary is punctuated by fearful references to Nazi treatment of Jews and dissidents.

LOYALTY AND BRAVERY

It was these qualities which made the Annexe a safe, secret and habitable place for over two years. Those who supported the Annexe inhabitants wittingly risked torture and death daily in order to bring food, which was vital, and also luxuries to keep their spirits up – books from Miep, a radio from Mr Kleiman, gifts on special occasions. The helpers never complain about the work or risk of caring for and protecting their friends, unless their protégés are careless and endanger them unnecessarily.

The most frequent helpers, Bep, Miep and Jan Gies, Mr Kugler and Mr Kleiman, exhibited enormous loyalty to their friends; there were many others, who may have had no personal relationship with those in the Annexe, who risked their safety in order to help, whether by illegally selling ration coupons, bringing vegetables or making repairs to the Annexe infrastructure.

Not least is the bravery of the Annexe inhabitants themselves who daily overcame their fear of arrest, often under very stressful conditions; they supported and encouraged each other and each found their own way to deal with the fear and isolation; before we condemn any behaviour which Anne writes about we must remember the extraordinarily frightening and difficult situation which would have been influencing their thoughts, feelings and actions.

ISOLATION

There are two forms of isolation in the diary: the general one, where the whole group has excluded itself from society for its own safety, and particular pockets of isolation, where individuals feel alone and misunderstood by others.

Adolescence can be a lonely time under any circumstances, but in the Annexe Anne experiences isolation from her contemporaries, from nature, from society and from her family with whom she has difficulty communicating as she moves from childhood into womanhood. She finds occasional relief in Peter and Margot, but neither fulfils her need for intimacy fully; only Kitty can but Kitty doesn't talk back.

Margot, Peter and even Bep have similar issues to deal with. Anne does not seem to consider the isolation of the adults, but assumes that it is easier for them; however we may assume that they also suffered in being isolated from society and friends, from loved ones (particularly Dussel) and in bearing the responsibility for the safety of the Annexe and the young people in it. Even the helpers would have experienced feelings of isolation in the enormity of the secret they had to keep and the responsibility for the lives of the Annexe inhabitants.

STRUCTURE

This is an intimate piece of personal writing, in diary form, in which a young adolescent girl expresses her private feelings, experiences, memories, hopes and despair, while trying to cope with the twin problems of confinement among people she does not particularly like and the onset of puberty. It is, therefore, not an uninterrupted narrative account but a fragmented record of her thoughts, emotions, opinions of others and herself and the day-to-day experiences in the Annexe.

It is, as far as Anne can make it, an honest account, for there would be no point in her trying to deceive herself. Though the main opinions expressed are, of necessity, Anne's own, at times we do hear the voices of the other inhabitants and their helpers.

A unity of sorts can be perceived in the universal
isolation of those in the Annexe, in the terror of
discovery they share with their helpers, in the mutual
difficulties of the adolescents, in the background of
the Second World War, the Holocaust and in the
constancy of their helpers. All these, threaded
throughout the diary, bind together otherwise disparate
pieces of writing. The ever-present figure of Anne and
her beloved Kitty serve the same purpose.

CHARACTERS

ANNE

Anne is a complex and fascinating girl, who carries
within herself the weight of irreconcilable
contradictions and a growing self-awareness. There
is a great need for her to share her feelings with a
confidant and, finding none, she expresses her feelings
to her diary.

We first see her as an attractive girl, popular with her
contemporaries. She has a number of suitors, whom she
deals with with light-hearted confidence. This attitude
(which she later perceives as frivolity) and her quick-
wittedness characterise her relationships before her
confinement.

Her strong character is reflected in the acceptance by
her peers of her leadership. Peter mentions that
whenever he has seen her, she has been the centre of

Quick-witted
Sensitive
Volatile
Studious
Articulate
Self-aware

attention. It is evidenced also by the way she is able to
deflect her teacher's attempts to control her gossiping
through setting punitive essays; by the letter she gives
her father declaring her independence and in the way
she confronts Mrs van Daan about her trying to flirt
with Otto.

The mischievous side of her character, appearing first
in the 'Chatterbox' essays, comes to the fore again

when she goads the adults into political arguments for her own amusement, puts hard brushes into Dussel's bed and posts Dussel's toilet schedule on the toilet door while he is inside. Her observations of the characters in the Annexe are often humorous or mischievous.

Anne's relationship with her parents before entering the Annexe has been good. Their concern is only for her health and happiness but she later blames them for spoiling her with kindness. In the confinement of the Annexe Anne begins to feel at odds with all her family. Anne believes her mother does not understand her and favours Margot. She relies on her father for protection and support, but finds it increasingly difficult to share her intimate feelings with him because he does not express his.

Anne and Edith disagree on most things. She cannot understand, herself, why she has such a violent antipathy towards her mother, but finds her advice and criticism unbearable. In her mind, Anne has concocted an ideal of motherhood and then castigates her mother for not attaining it. As she becomes a little more mature, she is appalled at what she has previously written abut her mother in her diary and has the integrity to confess that she could have seen no view but her own.

Anne targets Margot, too, at first placing her in the same category as her mother. She is jealous of what she sees as her parents' favouritism towards Margot. Nevertheless, Anne still describes Margot as 'perfection itself', without a trace of irony (see Literary Terms). As Anne matures she and Margot grow closer, communicating through notes, which are more comfortable than talking.

Anne needs love and her love for her father frequently bursts out in her writing. She respects him enormously and rarely does she feel at variance with him. Her arrogance in the letter she gives him soon subsides on hearing his view of how matters really are.

Anne finds Peter repulsive at first and her immediate need is for a female friend, but, in the circumstances, Peter will have to suffice. Her sensitivity to the sensibilities of others is apparent in the way she does not wish to be a nuisance to Peter. The awakening sexuality in each of them forms a bond between Peter and Anne. They each suffer the same adolescent turmoil of emotions: loneliness, vulnerability and lack of understanding from others. However, not even Peter is aware of the frantic, disorderly turbulence of emotions that sometimes drives Anne into a frenzy of frustration and helplessness. Anne empathises with Peter's loneliness and need to be loved. Though she is younger she wants to mother him. He can never be the true companion of her soul, since his shyness and sensitivity deter him from allowing Anne complete access to his deepest thoughts. At this stage, for Anne he is an obsession and she contemplates their relationship constantly. Peter is the first person with whom Anne can discuss and learn about sexual matters. Later, Anne begins to assert more control over her intimate relationship with Peter. The two young people are essentially different; Anne is idealistic, strong-willed, courageous, hard-working, religious, intelligent, none of which qualities are shared by Peter. Their mutual problems keep them together.

We have previously seen Anne's callous disregard for her mother's feelings, but in her relationship with Peter great sensitivity is evident. This same virtue is displayed in Anne's concern that Margot might be hurt by her relationship with Peter.

Without the distractions of friends and school, Anne is thrown entirely onto her own resources. The external frivolity has gone and Anne's serious inner life is taking over. Although she feels isolated Anne takes consolation from Kitty, from 'Petel', her imagined lover who will help her out, and from her friendship with Peter.

Anne is a hardworking girl. As soon as they arrive in the Annexe, she and Otto clear up the mess. Her study covers a wide expanse and depth of knowledge in which she is interested and involved. Only mathematics and monotonous work, like shelling peas, get her down.

Her intelligence is plain to see in the rational organisation of her thoughts as she expresses her opinions articulately to Kitty. She realises she is more intelligent that her mother and shows it in discussions. The annoyance she causes Dussel and Mrs van Daan has its roots in the fact that Anne is more intelligent than they are and makes them appear stupid. We know that she is intelligent also from her self-awareness, sensitivity and her imagination.

Anne has a love of Holland and its people, to such a degree that she intends to become a Dutch citizen after the war. In contrast, she considers the Germans enemy aliens and monsters, making no distinction between Germans and Nazis.

Anne's character is a profound mixture of many varied and at times opposing qualities that go to make up an endearing and poignant 'bundle of contradictions'. The last entry in her diary epitomises the two sides of Anne as she experiences them.

OTTO FRANK

Otto is everybody's anchor. It is he who has the foresight and organisational ability to plan the move to Holland as early as 1933. He prepares a place of refuge

Fair
Thoughtful
Generous
Intelligent

in the Annexe for his family and friends in advance of receiving the call-up notice.

In the first few pages of the diary, he twice receives the highest praise from Anne. His thoughtfulness is apparent in his bringing to the Annexe Anne's collection of pictures; he patches up the quarrel between Peter and his parents and while others complain about the food, Otto desires little for himself and shares his rations with Bep.

Anne admits she would be unable to cope if it were not for him. He defends her against Mrs van Daan's demands and then goes on the offensive against Mrs van Daan in his protection of Anne. He encourages and organises her education, which is a great safety valve for her, but he will not listen to Anne's criticism of her mother. He supports her in her visits to Peter and protects her diary.

Otto is a good guide to Anne, showing her how unjust she has been in the letter she has given him. He counsels Peter and Anne about their relationship in a kindly manner.

Everybody admires Otto and they express their appreciation of him in the birthday presents they give him. In his kindness, he presents gifts to all in return. At table, his concern is for everyone else and never for himself. People burden him with their troubles, for Anne tells us that he knows the 'intimate secrets' of many, but the stress he suffers himself has led him to attempt suicide, perhaps because he himself does not confide in others.

Otto is by no means a weak character. He disciplines Dussel when he breaks the safety rules and stops him when he tries to sabotage Anne's studies. During air raids, he is the only comfort Anne has and when there is a break-in, it is Otto that Peter goes to first, as the acknowledged leader, not to his father.

Otto's sensitivity is evident after Anne has refused to let her mother pray with her. He, who is so close to his daughter, avoids looking at her because of the distress he feels for her mother. The stress of having to arbitrate between the warring elements in the Annexe is etched on his face and he jumps whenever his name is called, at the prospect of having another problem to resolve.

An intelligent and educated man, Otto not only furthers his children's education but continues his own. He has all the qualities needed to help the small community to survive. He is the rock on whom they all depend.

EDITH HOLLANDER FRANK

Forthright
Religious
Concerned for her
children

We must remember with regard to Edith Frank that, at times, the picture Anne draws of her is, on her own admission, less than objective.

At first, we see her as a caring and lenient mother, concerned only for the health and happiness of her children, unworried about school reports. On entering the Annexe, however, she is exhausted and ignores the work that needs to be done, leaving it to Anne and Otto. In Anne's eyes she favours Margot and does not understand how her younger daughter feels. Hardly surprisingly, Edith does not treat thirteen-year-old Anne as an adult and the relationship of mother and daughter deteriorates.

Edith believes that you get on better in life by being forceful than you do from being retiring. In giving this advice to Anne, she is accused by Mrs van Daan of bringing up her children in a 'modern' way. Mrs Frank does not suffer fools gladly and tells Mrs van Daan exactly what she thinks of her claim to be modest. She is of a religious disposition and attempts to interest Anne in her German prayer book. Edith tries to avoid arguments if she can and says nothing about the van Daan's unequal distribution of food at breakfast. When life is difficult Edith's consolation is in contemplating all the worse suffering in the world whereas Anne finds consolation and hope in the beauty of nature.

Mrs Frank is a champion of the children's rights and always makes sure she wins their case for little extras. This would not seem to warrant the cruel rejection of her by Anne. Edith's hurt is visible in her demeanour.

There is a sense of balance in Edith's nature that differentiates her from Mrs van Daan. She has an excellent and detailed knowledge of all their provisions and shows an interest in the problems of teenagers in her reading, though Anne complains that this is purely theoretical. She can be over-sensitive sometimes and does have a trace of jealousy in her, because she does not like Anne talking more to Otto or Mrs van Daan than to her. She does also make the girls feel that they are under constant surveillance.

MARGOT FRANK

Margot is a brilliant student as her exam results testify. She seems not to have much energy or inclination for non-academic work, however, since on arrival at the Annexe she collapses onto a mattress while her father and younger sister do all the work of clearing up. She is sixteen years old and has a quiet, placid nature. At mealtimes she does not talk at all.

According to Anne, Margot is weak-willed and can always be persuaded by others. She is passive by nature, which might be the reason Dussel prefers her to Anne. On the other hand, she is kind and would like to help

Considerate
Highly intelligent
Placid

Anne out with her problems. It is obvious that she is concerned about her sister and observes her closely.

Calm as she is, Margot is irked by the close attention she receives from her parents, who take too seriously any action which varies from the norm, even though this concern is a sign of parental care. She, too, suffers from loneliness and the isolation that comes from having no girl friends of her own age. Though she feels this deeply, she is not jealous of Anne's association with Peter and is magnanimous enough to inform Anne of this.

Margot's ambition to nurse new-born babies shows a concern for and an interest in people rather than monetary gain and is entirely compatible with her unselfish nature.

PETER VAN DAAN

Peter is a shy boy who does not impress at first sight. Added to this, he is a hypochondriac who annoys Anne with his excessive worries about his health. For a boy of sixteen, he imagines he has a great number of health problems usually associated with greater age, such as lumbago and pains in his heart, kidneys and lungs. He has an insatiable appetite.

He is self-willed and retrieves an 'adult' book, which his father has confiscated once, causing a violent dispute. He can be rebellious and moody, as we see after this dispute.

Shy
Hypochondriac
Independent
Self-pitying
Thoughtful

Peter begins to be attracted to Anne and suffers from some of the same adolescent problems. Though he finds difficulty in expressing his thoughts because of his shyness, he has occasional outbursts. Initially, Peter expresses his feelings for Anne with meaningful looks and glances. He is short of affection and in need of friendship. Peter certainly gives Anne a great deal of understanding and companionship, and their friendship blossoms.

Peter has an ambition to emigrate to the Dutch East Indies after the war. He resents his Jewish birth and has a low self-esteem.

Peter feels the need for independence from his parents, but he thinks highly of Otto and is overwhelmed to learn that Otto likes him too. It is difficult for him to show his feelings, which he hides under a cloak of masculine indifference. He cannot entirely expose his inmost thoughts even to Anne, though he does come near to it by speaking intimately about his lack of trust in his family and about sexuality.

Peter is very hospitable and sensitive enough towards others to invite Margot as well as Anne to his room. Sometimes Anne believes Peter is the bravest of them all and he is a great comfort to her during a break-in and the subsequent air raid.

Otto agrees with Anne that Peter is a decent person but warns her that his character is weak. There is an aggressive side to him, but he is generally placid. One of his problems is his apathetic approach to his known weaknesses, when he ought to be fighting to overcome them. In spite of his earlier claim to wish to emigrate, he tends to lack ambition, is too dependent on Anne and full of self-pity.

PETRONELLA VAN DAAN

Argumentative Mrs van Daan loves an argument and has violent
Selfish altercations with her husband over trivia. She enjoys
Interfering goading her husband into a response and if no reaction
Highly strung occurs from one topic, she will quickly change to
Hard-working another. She also argues with Peter, Dussel, Anne, Edith and even, on occasion, Otto.

Selfishness is one of Petronella's worst traits. She removes most of her bed linen from their shared store, expecting Edith Frank to supply sheets for both families. When funds run low, Mr van Daan wishes to sell his wife's fur coat, but when he does so, Mrs van Daan wants to keep the money to buy clothes after the war.

Another problem Mrs van Daan has, according to Anne, is an inability to stop interfering in the upbringing of other people's children. She continually rebukes Anne for her non-stop talking and she reprimands her for not eating vegetables she dislikes. Her attacks on Anne do appear to be astonishingly vitriolic and vehement.

The accusation of stupidity levelled against Mrs van Daan would seem to be justified, as she proclaims before them all what a modest person she is and follows this up with a scathing attack on the way the Franks have brought up their children. Her violent, uncontrolled outbursts often strike Anne as comic. Mrs van Daan's comic behaviour is not confined only to the outpouring of enraged invective; it reaches its height in her attempts to flirt with Otto and Dussel.

Petronella is of an extremely nervous, as well as volatile disposition, and she therefore needs to be protected from the news that her furniture has been stolen from her home. She is more terrified than the others of burglars and air raids.

According to Anne, Mrs van Daan is two-faced and can be quite charming until one gets to know her. She tries to cause trouble within the Frank family and where food is concerned she is extremely greedy. Not only does she want the best for herself, but she and her husband are hiding food from the others. Her strengths seem to be that she is a good worker and, contrary to appearances, deeply in love with her husband.

Petronella is jealous of Mrs Frank when Mr Kugler gives her some extra sugar on her birthday. Her pettiness arises again as she objects to having a cake made for Mr Kugler's birthday. Her complaints cover so many aspects of her life that the rest cannot avoid laughing at her. Towards the end, she has lost all self-control and rages at everybody. She reaches the pitiful state of developing a toothache because Anne is having work done on her teeth. It can only be assumed that this is another example of her attention-seeking.

MR VAN DAAN

Opinionated
Disciplinarian
Greedy

Mr van Daan is a confrontational man, not only indulging in tempestuous arguments with his wife, but also brooking no contradiction of any opinion he has stated. He is a strict disciplinarian and a violent man, manifested in his treatment of Peter on occasions. He combines with his wife in trying to discipline Anne. With regard to his own well-being he is oversensitive and makes an immense fuss over having a cold.

Mr van Daan is under the delusion that he is an expert judge of politics. He is a greedy man at table. He infuriates Otto by hiding food from the Franks and Dussel as well. His attitude to Mr Dussel is one of confrontation or total ostracisation. He is as petty as his wife in objecting to the proposed cake for Mr Kugler.

MR DUSSEL

Petty
Inconsiderate
Self-centred
Opinionated
Meticulous

We know that he is meticulous and conscientious from the fact that he delays going into hiding in order to put his business affairs in order at his dental surgery. The first impression he makes is a good one.

Anne has to share her room with him, however, and soon discovers that he is inclined to criticise her faults

and relay them to her mother. The biscuits he promised
her never appear and he behaves in an inconsiderate
manner by putting the light on in Anne's room at dawn
in order to exercise.

A more serious matter is his disregard of the rules they
have set themselves for their own safety. Dussel's self-
centredness frequently endangers the lives of the
Annexe families. He persuades Miep to bring him a
banned book and Otto has to forbid him to write letters
to a number of people outside. His selfishness is proved
in his greed at table and when a secret food supply is
discovered in his cupboard. Coupled with this is an
acute meanness in giving nothing to the helpers, even
resenting Mr Kleiman the oranges he needs for his
sickness. Throughout the pages of Anne's diary Dussel
emerges as a petty, opinionated and disagreeable man.
Tension builds between he and Anne over the room
they share, over her study habits which he is dismissive
of, and over her way of being in general. He disagrees
with her opinions (on literature, on the war) but his
words often seem ill-considered, such as when he
claims that Hitler will fade from history, or calls Mrs
van Daan 'my child'; his words often cause hilarity.

Mr Dussel's strange sleeping habits are listed by Anne;
another eccentricity of his is to time Anne's clearing of
the table if he thinks she is a little late. When peeling
potatoes, he checks that everyone peels them the way
he does and lectures Anne because she does not. There
is something of the martinet in Mr Dussel. He presents
a comical figure with his flirtatious behaviour to Mrs
van Daan and even at his prayers.

Mr Dussel causes amusement with his lack of common
sense, vacillating views and absence of memory, but his
infuriating behaviour with the radio, which so upsets
Peter and Mr van Daan, brings home to the reader how

difficult he must have been to live with. Furthermore, his word cannot be trusted. His childish inability to obey regulations that are there to protect him brings a divide between himself and Otto, whom he insults. When it suits his purpose, he will make an abject show of apology, as he does to Mr van Daan the day before his birthday.

MIEP GIES
Trustworthy
Generous
Uncomplaining
Hard-working

From the beginning, Miep proves to be a trusted and trustworthy friend of the Franks, transporting clothing to their secret hiding place. Not only loyalty but also bravery is involved in such a mission.

In her kindness, she endeavours to protect the Annexe families from distressing news of the atrocities taking place outside against Jews. Her generosity is apparent also when she bakes a wonderful Christmas cake for them.

She is an invaluable help, shopping for them nearly every day and borrowing books for them from the public library. She even manages to provide Anne with shoes. Miep never complains about the danger she is exposed to or the trouble caused her by the needs of the refugees in the Annexe. Her affection, courage and loyalty are unquestioned.

At every opportunity, she is looking for means of helping the families, as the incident at the engagement party proves, when she takes note of the names and addresses of the two policemen in case they can be of future service. This occasion also provides us with an insight into another facet of her character – her usual moderation. At this celebration, she drinks and smokes, but this behaviour is unusual for Miep, whom Anne describes as their 'temperance advocate'. Otto has enough confidence in her to sign over his factory to her husband.

M̳r kleiman, mr kugler, bep and mr voskuijl

Courageous
Loyal
Kind
Cheerful

Mr Kleiman, Mr Kugler, Bep and her father play roles
as vital as that of Miep, but insufficient information is
present to write three extensive character sketches.
Nonetheless, it is important that they be recognised,
because they equally display qualities of kindness,
courage and loyalty and take identical risks. Anne pays
tribute to all of them and gives their qualities as
uncomplaining, cheerful, generous in their gifts, ever-
ready to do all they can.

They do indeed display a heroism equal to any on the
battlefield and they do it constantly.

L̳anguage and style

The language employed is simple, colloquial and
conversational, bringing an immediacy to the events
reported. It takes the form of a heart-to-heart talk with
an intimate friend and the device of personifying (see
Literary Terms) the diary as Kitty allows the reader to
be deceived into feeling that they are being addressed
personally and confidentially.

The piece is written in the first person, though direct
speech is introduced from time to time. The delivery is,
therefore, mainly subjective. There are times when
objectivity is aimed at, however. Anne acknowledges
that Mrs van Daan, whom she despises, has her good
points and is not always at fault. Anne also endeavours
to look at herself, at times, as though she is observing
someone else and is critical of her own work and
behaviour.

Anne's writing can be deeply personal and on a number
of occasions encompasses extremes of frustration,
despair and romanticism. Her style is honest and self-

aware. There is a frenzy in her writing when she tells of the frustration she feels because of her mother's 'mocking looks and accusations'. She uses the simile (see Literary Terms) of 'arrows from a tightly strung bow' to describe these barbs.

Her treatment of despair is equally moving, when she feels she cannot endure the atmosphere in the Annexe and the 'oppressive silence (that) clings to me as if it were going to drag me into the deepest regions of the underworld'. The impressive simile of the songbird, whose wings have been torn off, emphasises her hopelessness, as it crashes against the bars of its dark cage in a despairing attempt to escape.

Anne possesses a powerfully romantic streak and her never-forgotten dreams of Peter Schiff in January, somehow transferred onto Peter van Daan in April, so overwhelm her that she is incapable of expressing it fully and compresses all her emotion into the single word, 'Oh'.

Humour is interspersed throughout the diary, but on two occasions it appears in set pieces that could have come out of a play. Mrs van Daan's capering in the scene where she is undergoing dental treatment is masterly and would be wonderful on the stage. The same may be said of the occasion of Peter's proposed haircut, where there is a riot of action and emotion. The detail of the intimate group gathered around the radio listening to Winston Churchill, though not humorous, is dramatic and cleverly drawn.

Anne's descriptions are enhanced by the figurative language she uses. From the onomatopoeic (see Literary Terms) 'creaking of beds and sigh of broken springs' she moves to the understatement (litotes – see Literary Terms) of remarking that to be shot would be 'a fairly dismal prospect' and on to the ironic (see

Literary Terms) description of Mr van Daan as a
'revered gentleman' who has 'a great insight into
politics'. Not that all her language is so refined; her
description of bowel problems is decidedly earthy.

We are treated to homespun snippets of debatable
wisdom from time to time as Anne reflects on some
aspect of life. One of these is the fond belief that a
person with 'courage and faith will never die in misery'.
She tells us also that 'the young are lonelier than the
old', associating the old with her parents, who were in
their forties and fifties. She is closer to the mark with
her reflection on the meaning of love on page 200.

The great strength of Anne's writing lies in the her
ability to bring to life on the page herself and the
characters she tells us about. They are so real that we
feel we know them personally, which for a young girl of
her age is an immense achievement.

PART FOUR

STUDY SKILLS

HOW TO USE QUOTATIONS

One of the secrets of success in writing essays is the way you use quotations. There are five basic principles:

- Put inverted commas at the beginning and end of the quotation
- Write the quotation exactly as it appears in the original
- Do not use a quotation that repeats what you have just written
- Use the quotation so that it fits into your sentence
- Keep the quotation as short as possible

Quotations should be used to develop the line of thought in your essays.

Your comment should not duplicate what is in your quotation. For example:

Anne wants to be recognised as an individual, saying, 'I didn't want to be treated the same-as-all-the-other-girls, but as Anne-in-her-own-right'.

Far more effective is to write:

Anne demands to be treated not 'the same-as-all-the-other-girls, but as Anne-in-her-own-right'.

However, the most sophisticated way of using the writer's words is to embed them into your sentence:

Anne's wish is to be treated not in a general way but 'in-her-own-right'.

When you use quotations in this way, you are demonstrating the ability to use text as evidence to support your ideas - not simply including words from the original to prove you have read it.

Everyone writes differently. Work through the suggestions given here and adapt the advice to suit your own style and interests. This will improve your essay-writing skills and allow your personal voice to emerge.

The following points indicate in ascending order the skills of essay writing:
- Picking out one or two facts about the story and adding the odd detail
- Writing about the text by retelling the story
- Retelling the story and adding a quotation here and there
- Organising an answer which explains what is happening in the text and giving quotations to support what you write

....

- Writing in such a way as to show that you have thought about the intentions of the writer of the text and that you understand the techniques used
- Writing at some length, giving your viewpoint on the text and commenting by picking out details to support your views
- Looking at the text as a work of art, demonstrating clear critical judgement and explaining to the reader of your essay how the enjoyment of the text is assisted by literary devices, linguistic effects and psychological insights; showing how the text relates to the time when it was written

The dotted line above represents the division between lower- and higher-level grades. Higher-level performance begins when you start to consider your response as a reader of the text. The highest level is reached when you offer an enthusiastic personal response and show how this piece of literature is a product of its time.

Coursework essay

Set aside an hour or so at the start of your work to plan what you have to do.

- List all the points you feel are needed to cover the task. Collect page references of information and quotations that will support what you have to say. A helpful tool is the highlighter pen: this saves painstaking copying and enables you to target precisely what you want to use.

- Focus on what you consider to be the main points of the essay. Try to sum up your argument in a single sentence, which could be the closing sentence of your essay. Depending on the essay title, it could be a statement about a character: the first impression we are given of Peter is that he cannot be taken seriously because he is hypersensitive and lazy, but as time goes by Anne is drawn into intimacy with him because of their mutual need for a friend; an opinion about setting:Nobody would ever dream that there were so many rooms behind the drab, grey door. There is less chance still when the bookcase is built across it; or a judgement on a theme: Anne's relationship with her mother matures during their confinement. During the first months Anne can hardly stop herself from snapping back at her mother, yet a year later she exhibits more compassion and understanding.

- Make a short essay plan. Use the first paragraph to introduce the argument you wish to make. In the following paragraphs develop this argument with details, examples and other possible points of view. Sum up your argument in the last paragraph. Check you have answered the question.

- Write the essay, remembering all the time the central point you are making.

- On completion, go back over what you have written to eliminate careless errors and improve expression. Read it aloud to yourself, or, if you are feeling more confident, to a relative or friend.

If you can, try to type your essay, using a word processor. This will allow you to correct and improve your writing without spoiling its appearance.

Examination essay

The essay written in an examination often carries more marks than the coursework essay even though it is written under considerable time pressure.

In the revision period build up notes on various aspects of the text you are using. Fortunately, in acquiring this set of York Notes on *Anne Frank – The Diary of a Young Girl*, you have made a prudent beginning! York Notes are set out to give you vital information and help you to construct your personal overview of the text.

Make notes with appropriate quotations about the key issues of the set text. Go into the examination knowing your text and having a clear set of opinions about it.

In most English Literature examinations you can take in copies of your set books. This in an enormous advantage although it may lull you into a false sense of security. Beware! There is simply not enough time in an examination to read the book from scratch.

In the examination

- Read the question paper carefully and remind yourself what you have to do.
- Look at the questions on your set texts to select the one that most interests you and mentally work out the points you wish to stress.
- Remind yourself of the time available and how you are going to use it.
- Briefly map out a short plan in note form that will keep your writing on track and illustrate the key argument you want to make.
- Then set about writing it.
- When you have finished, check through to eliminate errors.

To summarise,
these are the
keys to success:

- **Know the text**
- **Have a clear understanding of and opinions on the storyline, characters, setting, themes and writer's concerns**
- **Select the right material**
- **Plan and write a clear response, continually bearing the question in mind**

Sample essay plan

A typical essay question on *Anne Frank – The Diary of a Young Girl* is followed by a sample essay plan in note form. This does not present the only answer to the question, merely one answer. Do not be afraid to include your own ideas and disregard some of those in the sample. Remember that quotations are essential to prove and illustrate the points you make.

'A study of teenage trauma.' How far do you agree with this assessment of Anne's diary?

Introduction

From the outset of the diary it is clear that, as a Jew, Anne's youth has been disrupted by Hitler's rule in Germany. Outline conditions faced by teenage characters in the diary.

Part 1

Elements of teenage trauma:
- Anne, Peter and Margot are all teenagers having to cope with immense difficulties
- Fear of persecution, discovery and arrest/death
- Trauma arising from isolation
- Owing to parents' lack of understanding
- Dichotomy of inner and external life
- Loneliness of unrequited longing for intimacy and love, independence and freedom.

Part 2

Balanced by light-heartedness:
- Happy scenes: dressing up and entertaining; celebrations of birthdays and feast-days

* Comic scenes: Dussel's dentistry; Peter's haircut
* the van Daans' arguments.

Part 3   Tyranny and persecution:
* a back-cloth to all the events in the diary, perpetually threatening to destroy them.

Give examples such as: helpers arrested; friends sent to concentration camps; break-ins; suspicious workers; building sold; Nazi news bulletins threatening Jews.

Part 4   Loyalty and bravery:
* devoted courage of helpers never wavers, even when some are arrested
* they give daily service despite their own problems
* they are constant, though the Annexe people put their lives in danger
* even people they do not know help them.

Part 5   Conclusion: a short summing up of points made and a statement of your final opinion with regard to the question.
For example:
* trauma of war is the backdrop to Anne's diary
* the teenagers experience adolescence in a most unusual and isolated environment
* in the diary there are few traumatic events, but the ongoing and occasionally highlighted fear of discovery, arrest and execution are deeply disturbing
* much of the trauma is the anticipation of disaster which Anne deals with remarkably; the reader may not be so well equipped as we know the tragic end to the diary and its author. The greatest trauma occurs when Anne and Kitty are separated.

You may wish to answer this question in a different fashion. This is merely an example of how it might be done.

1 To what extent is the diary objective in your opinion? Provide evidence from the text.
2 Discuss the main problems which affect Anne during her stay in the Annexe.
3 How does Anne depict the characters in such a realistic way? Support your answer by close reference to the diary.
4 From your reading of the diary, give your opinion on what you consider to be Anne's strengths and weaknesses. Give reasons for your opinion.
5 What evidence is there in the diary that Anne's picture of Mr Dussel is accurate?
6 'Anne is madly in love with Peter.' Agree or disagree, giving reasons from the diary for your opinion.
7 Peter states that his parents are very much in love. Can you find confirmation in the text of whether this is true or untrue? Support your answer by close reference to the diary.
8 How far do you consider Edith Frank to have been responsible for Anne's distress? Refer closely to the text in your answer.
9 Say who you feel are the outstanding people in this diary and demonstrate from the text the validity of your answer.
10 Choose the character you find most interests you and explain why, with detailed reference to the diary.

PART FIVE

CULTURAL CONNECTIONS

BROADER PERSPECTIVES

Some other books you might like to read about the holocaust are as follows:

The Hidden Children by Jane Marks. Twenty-three adults, who hid from the Nazis as children during World War I, tell moving tales of their experiences.

Have You Seen My Little Sister? by Janina Fischler-Martinho. The author tells how she, as a child, escaped from the Cracow Ghetto with her elder brother and of the loss of all the rest of her family.

Winter in the Morning by Janina Baumann. The author writes from her diaries of life in Warsaw when it was attacked by the Nazis, of the Jewish Ghetto there and her subsequent years in hiding.

After Long Silence by Helen Fremont. Helen was brought up a Catholic in America and discovered only in her thirties that her parents were Polish Jews. The story uncovers the horrors of their past.

There are many more books on the holocaust, which you can find on the internet at www.amazon.co.uk.

If you wish to know more about Anne Frank, there is a wonderful book called *Anne Frank the Biography* by Melissa Muller which contains all the details of her life. It brings you face to face with the people in the Annexe and all who were involved with Anne.

Film

There are no successful films of Anne Frank's diary to be recommended, but Sky TV have broadcast an excellent biography of Anne Frank, with contributions from Anne's friends, Hannah, Jacqueline and Hello Silberberg as well as from Miep Gies and Otto himself, if you wish to contact the company.

Schindler's List is a recent film which gives a chilling view of life under Nazi rule and of the lengths which people went to in order to protect Jews.

dramatic irony where the speaker does not understand the wider significance of his words but the reader does

irony words which say the opposite of what is meant

litotes understatement

onomatopoeia when the sound of the word echoes the sense – the 'sigh' of broken springs

personify to give a personality to something inanimate

metaphor where something is spoken of as though it were something else – planes 'sow' their bombs

simile a comparison of unlikely objects – accusations 'pierce like arrows'

TEST ANSWERS

TEST YOURSELF (Pages 1–66)

A 1 Hello Silberberg *(p. 15)*
2 Mr van Daan *(p. 31)*
3 Otto *(p. 43)*
4 Mrs van Daan *(p. 45)*

TEST YOURSELF (Pages 67–144)

A 1 Mr Dussel *(p. 69)*
2 Mrs van Daan *(p. 104)*
3 Mr Dussel *(p. 130)*
4 Mrs Frank *(p. 136)*
5 Margot *(p. 142)*

TEST YOURSELF (Pages 145–277)

A 1 Anne *(p. 157)*
2 Peter Schiff *(p. 162)*
3 Jan Gies *(p. 182)*
4 Mr van Daan *(p. 198)*
5 Peter van Daan *(p. 242)*
6 Anne *(p. 276)*

TEST YOURSELF (Pages 277–334)

A 1 Otto *(p. 282)*
2 Mrs van Daan *(p. 290)*
3 Mr van Daan *(p. 295)*
4 Peter and Margot *(p. 321)*
5 Margot *(p. 325)*
6 Otto *(p. 326)*

GCSE and equivalent levels (£3.50 each)

Maya Angelou
I Know Why the Caged Bird Sings

Jane Austen
Pride and Prejudice

Alan Ayckbourn
Absent Friends

Elizabeth Barrett Browning
Selected Poems

Robert Bolt
A Man for All Seasons

Harold Brighouse
Hobson's Choice

Charlotte Brontë
Jane Eyre

Emily Brontë
Wuthering Heights

Shelagh Delaney
A Taste of Honey

Charles Dickens
David Copperfield

Charles Dickens
Great Expectations

Charles Dickens
Hard Times

Charles Dickens
Oliver Twist

Roddy Doyle
Paddy Clarke Ha Ha Ha

George Eliot
Silas Marner

George Eliot
The Mill on the Floss

Anne Frank
The Diary of Anne Frank

William Golding
Lord of the Flies

Oliver Goldsmith
She Stoops To Conquer

Willis Hall
The Long and the Short and the Tall

Thomas Hardy
Far from the Madding Crowd

Thomas Hardy
The Mayor of Casterbridge

Thomas Hardy
Tess of the d'Urbervilles

Thomas Hardy
The Withered Arm and other Wessex Tales

L.P. Hartley
The Go-Between

Seamus Heaney
Selected Poems

Susan Hill
I'm the King of the Castle

Barry Hines
A Kestrel for a Knave

Louise Lawrence
Children of the Dust

Harper Lee
To Kill a Mockingbird

Laurie Lee
Cider with Rosie

Arthur Miller
The Crucible

Arthur Miller
A View from the Bridge

Robert O'Brien
Z for Zachariah

Frank O'Connor
My Oedipus Complex and Other Stories

George Orwell
Animal Farm

J.B. Priestley
An Inspector Calls

J.B. Priestley
When We Are Married

Willy Russell
Educating Rita

Willy Russell
Our Day Out

J.D. Salinger
The Catcher in the Rye

William Shakespeare
Henry IV Part 1

William Shakespeare
Henry V

William Shakespeare
Julius Caesar

William Shakespeare
Macbeth

William Shakespeare
The Merchant of Venice

William Shakespeare
A Midsummer Night's Dream

William Shakespeare
Much Ado About Nothing

William Shakespeare
Romeo and Juliet

William Shakespeare
The Tempest

William Shakespeare
Twelfth Night

George Bernard Shaw
Pygmalion

Mary Shelley
Frankenstein

R.C. Sherriff
Journey's End

Rukshana Smith
Salt on the Snow

John Steinbeck
Of Mice and Men

Robert Louis Stevenson
Dr Jekyll and Mr Hyde

Jonathan Swift
Gulliver's Travels

Robert Swindells
Daz 4 Zoe

Mildred D. Taylor
Roll of Thunder, Hear My Cry

Mark Twain
Huckleberry Finn

James Watson
Talking in Whispers

Edith Wharton
Ethan Frome

William Wordsworth
Selected Poems

A Choice of Poets

Mystery Stories of the Nineteenth Century including The Signalman

Nineteenth Century Short Stories

Poetry of the First World War

Six Women Poets

York Notes Advanced (£3.99 each)

Margaret Atwood
Cat's Eye

Margaret Atwood
The Handmaid's Tale

Jane Austen
Mansfield Park

Jane Austen
Persuasion

Jane Austen
Pride and Prejudice

Alan Bennett
Talking Heads

William Blake
Songs of Innocence and of Experience

Charlotte Brontë
Jane Eyre

Emily Brontë
Wuthering Heights

Angela Carter
Nights at the Circus

Geoffrey Chaucer
The Franklin's Prologue and Tale

Geoffrey Chaucer
The Miller's Prologue and Tale

Geoffrey Chaucer
Prologue To the Canterbury Tales

Geoffrey Chaucer
The Wife of Bath's Prologue and Tale

Samuel Taylor Coleridge
Selected Poems

Joseph Conrad
Heart of Darkness

Daniel Defoe
Moll Flanders

Charles Dickens
Great Expectations

Charles Dickens
Hard Times

Emily Dickinson
Selected Poems

John Donne
Selected Poems

Carol Ann Duffy
Selected Poems

George Eliot
Middlemarch

George Eliot
The Mill on the Floss

T.S. Eliot
Selected Poems

F. Scott Fitzgerald
The Great Gatsby

E.M. Forster
A Passage to India

Brian Friel
Translations

Thomas Hardy
The Mayor of Casterbridge

Thomas Hardy
The Return of the Native

Thomas Hardy
Selected Poems

Thomas Hardy
Tess of the d'Urbervilles

Seamus Heaney
Selected Poems from Opened Ground

Nathaniel Hawthorne
The Scarlet Letter

Kazuo Ishiguro
The Remains of the Day

Ben Jonson
The Alchemist

James Joyce
Dubliners

John Keats
Selected Poems

Christopher Marlowe
Doctor Faustus

Arthur Miller
Death of a Salesman

John Milton
Paradise Lost Books I & II

Toni Morrison
Beloved

Sylvia Plath
Selected Poems

Alexander Pope
Rape of the Lock and other poems

William Shakespeare
Antony and Cleopatra

William Shakespeare
As You Like It

William Shakespeare
Hamlet

William Shakespeare
King Lear

William Shakespeare
Measure for Measure

William Shakespeare
The Merchant of Venice

William Shakespeare
A Midsummer Night's Dream

William Shakespeare
Much Ado About Nothing

William Shakespeare
Othello

William Shakespeare
Richard II

William Shakespeare
Romeo and Juliet

William Shakespeare
The Taming of the Shrew

William Shakespeare
The Tempest

William Shakespeare
Twelfth Night

William Shakespeare
The Winter's Tale

George Bernard Shaw
Saint Joan

Mary Shelley
Frankenstein

Jonathan Swift
Gulliver's Travels and A Modest Proposal

Alfred, Lord Tennyson
Selected Poems

Alice Walker
The Color Purple

Oscar Wilde
The Importance of Being Earnest

Tennessee Williams
A Streetcar Named Desire

John Webster
The Duchess of Malfi

Virginia Woolf
To the Lighthouse

W.B. Yeats
Selected Poems

NOTES